Presented to:

_____

From:

_____

Date:

_____

Mothers who made a Difference

SEEMINGLY INSIGNIFICANT ACTS THAT CHANGED THE WORLD

MICHELLE COX

HONOR HB BOOKS

Inspiration and Motivation for the Seasons of Life

COOK COMMUNICATIONS MINISTRIES
Colorado Springs, Colorado • Paris, Ontario
KINGSWAY COMMUNICATIONS LTD
Eastbourne, England

Honor® is an imprint of
Cook Communications Ministries, Colorado Springs, CO 80918
Cook Communications, Paris, Ontario
Kingsway Communications, Eastbourne, England

MOTHERS WHO MADE A DIFFERENCE
© 2007 Michelle Cox

The Web addresses (URLs) recommended throughout this book are solely offered as a resource to the reader. The citation of these Web sites does not in any way imply an endorsement on the part of the author or the publisher, nor does the author or publisher vouch for their content for the life of this book.

First printing, 2007
Printed in the United States of America

1 2 3 4 5 6 7 8 9 10

Cover Design: LJDesigns
Cover Photo: Royalty Free, © Photodisc
Interior Design: YaYe Design
Interior Photos: © Photodisc, © Thinkstock

All Scripture quotations are taken from the New King James Version. Copyright © 1982 by Thomas Nelson, Inc. Used by permission. All rights reserved.

ISBN 978-1-56292-837-7

Dedicated with love to my husband, Paul—my sweetheart, my best friend, and my biggest cheerleader

To my sons, Jeremy, Tim, and Jason—the joy of my life

To my daughters-in-law, Lydia and Laurel—the answer to a mother's prayers

Ideals and principles continue from generation to generation only when they are built into the hearts of children as they grow up.

—George S. Benson

Contents

Foreword

I N MARCH OF 1975, I began my journey of ministry by serving as youth pastor at Trinity Baptist Church in Asheville, North Carolina. Thirty-one years later, I am now the senior pastor of the church.

After salvation and discipleship, I have observed two factors that help to determine the outcome of a life. One is the factor of family, and the other is the factor of faithfulness. A life lacking the example of either factor is handicapped at best.

Michelle Cox writes for you with the added blessing of both life-building factors of family and faithfulness. She and her husband, Paul, were young teens in our church thirty-one years ago when I began my ministry. I've watched them grow from teens to young adults who married and have faithfully served the Lord.

As the mother of three sons, Michelle has experienced the power of a mom who's been used by God to form a family and to instill the great trait of being faithful.

God has asked you to be a mother. Your faithfulness will affect your family as you answer God's special calling to mold and shape the world we wait in for his Son's return.

God has given Michelle a great insight about motherhood that will be a blessing to you as you read *Mothers Who Made a Difference*. Don't miss this opportunity from Michelle's heart and pen.

Respectfully,
Ralph H. Sexton Jr.
Senior Pastor
Trinity Baptist Church

Acknowledgments

A BOOK DOESN'T HAPPEN WITHOUT the help and cooperation of many people and I'm grateful for this opportunity to thank the special individuals who have been part of this project.

My deepest appreciation to Jeff Dunn, Ingrid Beck, Jon Woodhams, and everyone at Cook Communications Ministries/Honor Books who helped *Mothers Who Made a Difference* become a reality.

Thank you to my mentor, author and conference director Yvonne Lehman. I can never repay you for sharing your time and your talent to help a beginning writer. You are a special friend and I'm grateful God put you in my life. He has used you and the Blue Ridge Mountains Christian Writers Conference (www.lifeway.com/christianwriters) to open doors for my writing. The idea for *Mothers Who Made a Difference* occurred at your conference.

I am indebted to Jerry B. Jenkins, and the wonderful staff at the Christian Writers Guild. This book would not be in existence without you! The Writing for the Soul Conference (www.christianwritersguild.com) provided the contact with Jeff Dunn that resulted in the contract for this book.

Special appreciation goes to Margaret Skiles for encouragement, grammar assistance, and the gift of complete honesty. You made my work better.

My writers group—Yvonne Lehman, Ann Tatlock, Debbie Presnell, Lisa Wilson, and Aileen Lawrimore—has been invaluable throughout this process. Thank you for your suggestions, corrections, laughter, and friendship. You're the best.

I send a huge thank-you to my prayer team: Lorraine Sherlin, Lavonia Whitson, Doug Guy, Margaret Skiles, Terry McCoy, Debbie McCoy, Luke McCoy, Dianne Waggoner, Mary Jane Hollyday, John Perrodin, Debbie Presnell, Connie Norris, the Trinity Baptist Singles, and my family. You are the strength behind my writing and I could not do this without you. God bless you for your faithfulness.

Thank you to Dr. Bill Day, Bible scholar and president of the Trinity Baptist Bible College, for taking the time to read my manuscript.

Special appreciation goes to my writing buddy, John Perrodin, for his insight, critiques, and encouragement as I worked on this book.

Thank you to the friends and family who were kind enough to share their stories. I know God will use your experiences to touch hearts and lives.

I would be remiss if I didn't thank my husband and children for their love and support, and for pitching in around the house during those days when it seemed as though I lived at the computer. Thanks for your patience. I love you!

Last but not least, thank you to the God who gave me the dream and then equipped me with what I needed to accomplish the task.

Introduction

URING A DEVOTIONAL SESSION at the Blue Ridge Mountains Christian Writers Conference, the speaker mentioned that her Bible study group was studying the story of the little lad with his five loaves and two fish. One of the women in her group asked the question, "Wonder where the mama was?"

I had never thought about that aspect before and the thought kept whirling through my head while I drove home from the conference. I was touched as I realized something that is an encouragement every time I think about it: Because a mother did something ordinary—because she packed a lunch with five loaves and two fish—her child was part of a miracle.

How well I remember the days when my three sons were little. I loved being a mom, but there were days when exhaustion led to discouragement and a feeling of insignificance. I certainly didn't feel as if my tasks as a mom were instruments of greatness for God. How wonderful to realize that God can take something as ordinary as packing a lunch, baking a pan of bread, or making a basket and use it for his glory. That is the concept for *Mothers Who Made a Difference: Seemingly Insignificant Acts That Changed the World.*

This book features the stories of eight contemporary mothers and eight Bible mothers. While the Bible gives little detail about some of these women, I'm certain God included these mothers in the Bible for a reason. I have attempted to get inside their hearts and to tell their stories as they might have been. As you read the stories, I think you'll be amazed at the relevance of their life experiences to our lives as women today.

My hope is that God will use this book to encourage your heart and to recharge your "mom batteries." Always remember that God values your efforts. He can use your ordinary tasks as a mom in extraordinary ways, and he will be with you for every step of the parenting journey.

I'd love to hear from you if *Mothers Who Made a Difference* has touched your heart and life in any way. Come visit with me at my Web site:

www.michellecoxinspirations.com.

1

Because a Mother Made a Basket

A Mother's Story

I COULD TELL DEBBIE was crying when I answered the phone. Her stark words stunned me. "Teresa has breast cancer. The doctors are going to do a mastectomy and they've scheduled surgery for next week."

I remember glancing out the sliding glass door at the bright sunshine. How could the sun still be shining when the situation had become so dark for Teresa? It's odd how one notices things like that when a loved one's world falls apart.

My husband and I worked with our church youth group. We first met Teresa when she came as a guest with her friend Debbie. Over the next few years, we watched her become a vibrant, beautiful woman with the touch of God on her life.

> *How could the sun still be shining when the situation had become so dark for Teresa?*

Everyone she met fell in love with her sunny personality. She traveled, had a great job, wonderful friends, and stylish clothes. Her life seemed almost perfect—until this disaster struck.

The scheduled surgery date arrived. She did well through the procedure and we were encouraged when the doctors seemed optimistic for her future. Weeks of chemo followed the surgery and we ached for Teresa when she experienced nausea and extreme fatigue. We cried with her when the day she had dreaded arrived, and her gorgeous hair fell out in clumps. She was stronger than we were, and we were awed by her courage and inspired by her unwavering faith that God was in control of her situation.

> *God was in control of her situation.*

The months passed and Teresa's life slowly returned to normal. Her hair grew back and we were thrilled to see the vibrant young woman we loved feeling energetic and looking healthy again.

Things seemed to be going well for her. She was back at work and traveling again. She began dating and we watched with delight as the relationship became serious.

We cried with joy at Teresa and Kenny's wedding. Months later when she announced she was

expecting a baby, we were ecstatic. All her dreams were finally coming true.

Then disaster struck again. In the midst of her pregnancy, the cancer returned. It was aggressive and the doctors had no choice but to move ahead with immediate surgery to remove the remaining breast.

More than thirty of us sat in the hospital waiting room during Teresa's surgery praying for her and her unborn child. A collective sigh of relief filled the room when the doctor walked in and reported, "We think we got all the cancer. Her pregnancy should go smoothly now and we think the baby will be fine."

Jacob's birth was the bright spot following those scary months and we treasured Teresa's joy. The one thing she had always wanted was to be a mother and she cherished every moment with her tiny son.

We had never seen her look better. Motherhood definitely suited her and she glowed with happiness.

The months passed. She continued with regular checkups and we celebrated as each visit went by with no new problems. Life went back to normal and everything seemed to be going well.

> *Life went back to normal and everything seemed to be going well.*

Then she began having severe headaches. At first, the doctors thought she was having cluster migraines but further tests revealed that wasn't the problem.

The news was bad.

The doctors found six brain tumors and the prognosis wasn't good. Deep down, even though we didn't want to admit it, we knew we were no longer dealing with healing for Teresa, now we were dealing with quality of life for the time she had left.

Debbie called. "Teresa's asking for you. Can you come?"

Her only request was that I pray for her family.

"Of course," I responded, and we set a date for the next morning.

Praying for strength, I walked into her house and reached to hug her. We cried together and then settled down to talk. Jacob toddled into the room and climbed onto her lap. My heart shattered while I watched her hug him close, clutching him as if she could squeeze a lifetime of a mother's love into the short time she had left.

We talked about her diagnosis and the doctor's plan for treatment. Then I asked, "Teresa, what can I do to help you get through this? You know I'll do anything for you."

Her only request was that I pray for her family. "God's given me peace about this and I'm okay, but my family is really hurting. Will you pray that God will comfort their hearts?"

And this was *her* prayer: "God, you gave me this

child and he's so precious to me. I know I won't be there to watch Jacob grow, so will you make sure he's always loved and please take care of him for me? I place him in your hands."

From then until the day God called her to heaven, she rested in the fact that there's no safer place on the face of the earth than placing one's child in God's hands. However, her going home to heaven was not the end of Teresa's story.

Her death was heartbreaking for all of us who loved her and we mourned her loss. We grieved even more when we looked at her precious little boy who no longer had a mother to hold him on her lap or to comfort him when he was hurt. We knew how much Teresa had wanted to be there for Jacob's first day of school, to celebrate his birthdays, to cheer at his graduation, and to see him walk down the aisle on his wedding day. But God had other plans.

Fast-forward several years and a special woman named Glenda unexpectedly entered Kenny and Jacob's lives, first falling in love with little Jacob and then with Kenny.

We're convinced Glenda was handpicked from heaven.

Over the last few years, we've observed Glenda's loving care for Jacob. Her sweet spirit has touched us, as she's become a caring mother to Jacob, while at

> *There's no safer place on the face of the earth than placing one's child in God's hands.*

the same time making every effort to keep Teresa's memory alive for him. We're convinced Glenda was handpicked from heaven.

Those of us who loved Teresa are comforted knowing that God answered a mother's heartfelt prayers for someone to love her child. And we're convinced beyond a doubt that placing her child in God's hands was the wisest decision Teresa ever made.

> *I have held many things in my hand and lost them all, but whatever I have placed in God's hands, that I always possess.*
>
> —Martin Luther

Straight from Scripture

NOW THERE AROSE a new king over Egypt, who did not know Joseph. And he said to his people, "Look, the people of the children of Israel *are* more and mightier than we; come, let us deal shrewdly with them, lest they multiply, and it happen, in the event of war, that they also join our enemies and fight against us, and *so* go up out of the land."

Therefore they set taskmasters over them to afflict them with their burdens. And they built for Pharaoh supply cities, Pithom and Raamses.

But the more they afflicted them, the more they multiplied and grew. And they were in dread of the children of Israel.

So the Egyptians made the children of Israel serve with rigor.

And they made their lives bitter with hard bondage—in mortar, in brick, and in all manner of service in the field. All their service in which they made them serve *was* with rigor....

So Pharaoh commanded all his people, saying, "Every son who is born you shall cast into the river, and every daughter you shall save alive...."

And a man of the house of Levi went and took as *wife* a daughter of Levi.

So the woman conceived and bore a son. And when she saw that he *was* a beautiful *child*, she hid him three months.

But when she could no longer hide him, she took an ark of bulrushes for him, daubed it with asphalt and pitch, put the child in it, and laid *it* in the reeds by the river's bank. And his sister stood afar off, to know what would be done to him.

Then the daughter of Pharaoh came down to bathe at the river. And her maidens walked along the riverside; and when she saw the ark among the reeds, she sent her maid to get it.

And when she opened *it*, she saw the child, and behold, the baby wept. So she had compassion on him, and said, "This is one of the Hebrews' children."

Then his sister said to Pharaoh's daughter, "Shall I go and call a nurse for you from the Hebrew women, that she may nurse the child for you?"

And Pharaoh's daughter said to her, "Go." So the maiden went and called the child's mother.

Then Pharaoh's daughter said to her, "Take this child away and nurse him for me, and I will give *you* your wages." So the woman took the child and nursed him. (Ex. 1:8–14, 22; 2:1–9)

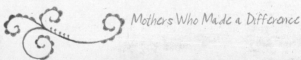

Mothers Who Made a Difference

Mothers of the Bible

JOCHEBED WAS SO TIRED of being pregnant. Her back ached, her feet were swollen, and she was huge. A dark depression engulfed her—but not from her physical ailments. She simply did not want this baby. Somehow she knew it was going to be a boy and she did not want to have this baby!

She had experienced childbirth before and had eagerly anticipated the pleasure of a child nestled in her arms. She had inhaled the sweet aroma of a fresh-bathed baby and felt the texture of downy hair and soft skin. She had known the indescribable love for a child that floods a mother's heart.

This time was different. Jochebed did not want *this* child.

She hadn't slept well since the day she learned she was pregnant. Her nights were consumed with nightmares too horrible to consider in the bright light of day. Night after night she whimpered in her sleep, tortured by the mental picture of her baby sinking below the surface of the water while she stood helplessly on the banks of the river.

Other nights her slumber allowed her mind to go one step further and she would wake screaming, her mind filled with the vivid image of her baby son pinned by the sharp teeth and strong jaws of a crocodile as it submerged into the murky depths of the river.

Nine months had never before seemed so long.

A sharp pain racked through her abdomen, doubling her over with its force. Her time had come. Catching her breath, she beckoned her daughter. "Miriam, get your father and then find the midwife. The baby is coming." *Oh, please, God. Don't let it be a boy!*

Oh, please, God. Don't let it be a boy!

Her husband entered the room and she grabbed him in a panic. "Oh, Amram, the baby is coming. What if it's a boy? What are we going to do?"

There wasn't an answer, and all he could do was pull her into his arms and hold her while his tears joined hers.

The afternoon seemed to last forever. Finally, the cry of a healthy baby filled the small home. Out of habit, the midwife bathed the newborn babe and wrapped a clean cloth around the tiny body.

Jochebed grasped her husband's arm and nervously asked, "Is it a boy or a girl? Tell me it's a girl."

Amram quietly choked out, "It's a boy."

Tears streamed down Jochebed's face, but they weren't tears of joy. She knew this innocent Hebrew baby boy had an instant death sentence placed on his little head.

"Let me see the baby," Jochebed whispered.

Amram gently placed him in her arms. Through a haze of tears, she counted his tiny fingers and toes. She held him to her shoulder and his little head nestled against her neck. Despite her intentions of distancing herself from this child, her heart flooded with love.

The midwife mumbled, "You know what we have to do. I wish it could be different, but I am commanded to remind you of Pharaoh's order that every son born to a Hebrew woman must be thrown in the river."

Clutching the child protectively to her chest, Jochebed cried, "No! He's so precious." Turning him so the midwife could see him, she cried, "He's a beautiful baby. Look at him! Please don't make me do this."

Despite her intentions of distancing herself from this child, her heart flooded with love.

With tears dripping off his cheeks, Amram whispered, "Honey, I want to keep him too, but we don't have a choice. We have to follow Pharaoh's orders."

Hysteria tinged Jochebed's voice as she pleaded with the midwife, "You know what it's like to be a mother. Can you imagine putting *your* baby in the river to die? Please, help me keep this a secret—just for a few months. He's so precious. Look at him!"

The midwife's gaze fell upon the newborn sleeping in his mother's arms. She flinched, turned, and began gathering her supplies. "I'll keep your secret, but you know you can't keep him. If Pharaoh learns of this, there will be dire consequences for all of us."

Knowing their days were numbered, each day with her son was precious for Jochebed. Then three months later, the time arrived when there was no longer any choice—they *had* to follow Pharaoh's orders.

Amram asked, "What are you doing?"

Jochebed replied, "I'm not just throwing this child in the river to die. I'm making a basket for him. God's in control of the situation and I'm going to trust him to do what's best."

> God's in control of the situation.

She had made many baskets, but she wove this one with special care. She knew the possibility was real that this might be the final resting place for her baby boy.

Waterproofing was crucial, and she carefully coated the basket with asphalt and pitch—and her tears.

Finally, the time arrived when she could put it off no longer. She gathered her precious child in her arms, clutching him to her as if she could squeeze a lifetime of a mother's love into just a few short moments. *God, why did you let him be born— only to die?*

She stroked his downy head, inhaled that wonderful aroma distinctive to babies, traced the outline of his little hands, and reached to kiss his soft cheek just one last time. Then she placed his tiny body into the basket.

She reached to kiss his soft cheek just one last time.

And this was her prayer. "God, you gave me this child and he's so precious to me. I know I won't be there to watch him grow, so will you make sure he's always loved and please take care of him for me? I place him in your hands."

Lifting the basket, she slowly walked outside. "Miriam, come with me to the river."

When they arrived at the water's edge, she placed the basket in the reeds lining the river, then turned and blindly stumbled up the bank. "Miriam, I can't watch. Stay and see what happens to him."

Later that day, Pharaoh's daughter came to the river to bathe. Noticing the basket floating in the water, she sent her maids to collect it. When they opened the basket, the baby began to cry—as if on

cue from God—and the heart of Pharaoh's daughter melted. "This must be one of the Hebrews' children," she guessed.

When Miriam saw the tender look on the face of Pharaoh's daughter, she immediately asked, "Would you like me to find one of the Hebrew women to come nurse the child for you?"

"Go," Pharaoh's daughter replied, and Miriam instantly ran to find her mother.

"Mama," she yelled, and Jochebed started running to her, piteous tears streaking down her cheeks.

"Oh, Miriam, is it over? What happened? Is he … dead? No … I don't want to know."

"Mama, don't cry. It's good news! Come and see."

When Jochebed arrived at the river, Pharaoh's daughter said, "Take this child with you and nurse him. I will pay you for your trouble."

And Jochebed took baby Moses home with the certain knowledge that there's no safer place on the face of the earth than placing one's child in God's hands.

Application

ERESA AND JOCHEBED faced scary circumstances that were out of their control. Both of them were wise enough to trust God during those tough times and both learned that the safest place for one's child is in God's hands.

Ask yourself:

1. What scary or tough situations am I facing as a mom?
2. How do I respond to those circumstances?
3. Do I trust God, or am I trying to solve the problems myself?
4. Have I consciously placed my child in God's hands?

Dear Lord,

As I face tough situations in my life, remind me to trust in you, knowing that I can always count on you to be faithful. Thank you for the gift of my child. I place this precious child in your hands, realizing that there's no safer place on the face of the earth. Help me to be the mother I desire to be, and help my child to see you in me. *Amen.*

Reflections

USE THIS SPACE TO RESPOND to the stories or to answer the questions.

_____

_____

_____

_____

_____

_____

_____

_____

_____

_____

_____

_____

_____

_____

_____

_____

_____

_____

_____

_____

_____

_____

_____

_____

_____

_____

_____

_____

_____

_____

_____

_____

_____

_____

_____

2

Because a
Mother
Baked
Some
Bread

A Mother's Story

I SLOWLY OPENED THE PANTRY door and surveyed the contents. Tears welled in my eyes and the knot in my stomach tightened another notch at the sight of the few cans and boxes left on the shelves.

I remembered the days I had taken for granted, days when the pantry shelves had been filled to capacity. Now the basic essentials were almost gone and snack foods and luxury items were but a distant memory.

Things were desperate and I wondered how I could continue to feed my family.

My heart broke each time my children asked for a bag of cookies or a favorite box of cereal. My husband and I had pinched pennies until there was nothing left to pinch. Things were desperate and I wondered how I could continue to feed my family with the scanty supply of items left on the shelves.

"God, what are we going to do? I don't understand. We've been faithful to you and to church. We've given our tithes. We're trying to raise our children for you. Doesn't that count for anything? God, don't you care? I feel like you're a million miles away." A tear of pain—and yes, anger—slipped down my cheek.

We hadn't done anything to cause this situation. We hadn't been poor money managers and we hadn't spent our money foolishly. My husband was a building contractor and operated his own business. From the day we were married he had been a hard worker and a good provider for his family.

He had spent several months working on various construction projects and had invested our savings in the building materials that were needed to complete the jobs.

Then, in a series of domino-like chain reactions, our financial situation fell apart. First, a contractor withheld payment because the building's owners had not paid him, then a home owner's check bounced, and then another contractor went bankrupt without paying us for the materials or the work my husband had completed.

God, don't you care? I feel like you're a million miles away.

Now, due to circumstances beyond his control, we were in big trouble.

Of course, that was the week the motor in my husband's truck went out, with the verdict that the motor would have to be rebuilt. We thought things surely couldn't get any worse, but we soon discovered they could as the transmission went out in my car, the dishwasher started leaking, the washer quit working, and the television died.

> *We thought things surely couldn't get any worse, but we soon discovered they could.*

I ached as I watched my husband's pain, his loss of self-esteem during those difficult days of trying to pay the bills and put food on the table for his family.

Turning from the pantry, I walked by the row of cookbooks in the kitchen. Angry and frustrated, I muttered, "Maybe someone should write a cookbook called *How to Make Something Out of Nothing*."

The next day, fighting back tears, I trudged through the grocery store while my husband waited in the car with the children. I passed the containers of fresh strawberries, inhaling their aroma and giving them a wistful glance as I thought about how much I'd love to buy some for my family.

Walking to a deserted corner of the store, I removed the billfold from my purse and carefully counted the few bills and coins inside as if they might miraculously have reproduced. Nope, there was still only six dollars—six measly dollars to buy enough groceries to last several days.

I tasted the sharp tang of blood from where I had bitten the inside of my cheek to hold back the tears. I carefully added the figures as I wearily placed a bag of pinto beans, a loaf of bread, a box of powdered milk, and a jar of off-brand peanut butter into the buggy.

Fear overwhelmed me, making it difficult to draw a deep breath. Standing in the middle of the store I inwardly screamed, "God, where are you when I need you? Don't you care that my family will soon be starving?"

Then as clear as if I had heard the words spoken aloud, the reply from heaven came, "I have everything under control and I'll supply your need. Just trust me."

A sweet, unexplainable peace filled my soul. No, the circumstances hadn't changed, but the assurance that God was in control of our situation made all the difference.

A sweet, unexplainable peace filled my soul.

Tears were dripping from my cheeks as I climbed into the car holding my little bag of groceries.

"Honey, are you okay?" my husband questioned as he reached to hug me, a look of pain evident on his face. "Things are going to get better."

I finally choked out, "I know they are. That's

Mothers Who Made a Difference

why I'm crying. God just gave me the assurance that he has everything under control. I don't know how he's going to do it, but he's going to take care of us, and everything's going to be okay."

And the first evidence of God's provision came the next morning, as an unexpected refund check for $75.00 arrived in the mail.

> *The first evidence of God's provision came the next morning.*

> *When you have nothing left but God ... you become aware that God is enough.*
> —A. Maude Royden

Straight from Scripture

HEN THE WORD of the LORD came to him, saying, "Arise, go to Zarephath, which *belongs* to Sidon, and dwell there. See, I have commanded a widow there to provide for you."

So he arose and went to Zarephath. And when he came to the gate of the city, indeed a widow *was* there gathering sticks. And he called to her and said, "Please bring me a little water in a cup, that I may drink."

And as she was going to get *it*, he called to her and said, "Please bring me a morsel of bread in your hand."

So she said, "As the LORD your God lives, I do not have bread, only a handful of flour in a bin, and a little oil in a jar; and see, I *am* gathering a couple of sticks that I may go in and prepare it for myself and my son, that we may eat it, and die."

And Elijah said to her, "Do not fear; go *and* do as you have said, but make me a small cake from it first, and bring *it* to me; and afterward make *some* for yourself and your son.

"For thus says the LORD God of Israel: 'The bin of flour shall not be used up, nor shall the jar of oil run dry, until the day the LORD sends rain on the earth.'"

So she went away and did according to the word of Elijah; and she and he and her household ate for *many* days.

The bin of flour was not used up, nor did the jar of oil run dry, according to the word of the LORD which He spoke by Elijah. (1 Kings 17:8–16)

Mothers Who Made a Difference

Mothers of the Bible

CLOUDS OF DUST SWIRLED through the air with each step the widow of Zarephath took through the yard. She wiped a hand across her face feeling the rough graini-ness of the dust particles on her skin. Depression settled over her as she surveyed the barren landscape. Everything living and green had disap-peared and there were only brown stubs and withered stalks where vegetation had once flourished.

The weight of the responsibility caused her shoulders to sag.

Drought had settled on the land and famine quickly followed. Problems that once seemed large suddenly shrank in significance as the life and death issues of finding food and water took precedence.

What am I going to do? The weight of the respon-sibility caused her shoulders to sag. *Oh, what I'd give if* my husband were here to help carry this burden, to put his arms around me and tell me that everything is going to be okay. A slow tear trickled down her cheek as a fresh wave of grief washed over her.

The days were so lonely without him. The nights were even worse. Those were the hours when all her fears and inadequacies crept into the room, stealing her sleep and leaving her drained and exhausted for the next day.

She still slept with his cloak, hugging it to her each nof shared laughter while watching their son play. As the months went by, the scent was fading from the cloak, just as the memories were fading in height like a security blanket, inhaling the faint aroma of her husband that still clung to the fabric. Sometimes she closed her eyes and pretended he was still there, Then the heartbreaking reality would seep into her soul. *He's gone and he'll never be back.* No more hugs. No more sweet kisses. No more evenings mind. *I'm afraid I'll forget what you looked like, the sound of your laughter, the rough feel of your cheek against mine, the loving expression on your face as you played with our son.*

Don't you know I can't do this without you?

"How could you leave me like this?" she muttered angrily, spasms of weeping bending her double.

Mothers Who Made a Difference

"I feel like my heart has been ripped in half. Don't you know I can't do this without you? I'm so tired of carrying this burden alone and now I'm failing you and our son. I can't even provide enough food for us."

"Mother, where are you?" The sound of her son's voice penetrated her consciousness.

> *She bent and drew him close for a hug, drawing comfort from the little arms.*

"I'm outside, Son. I'll be inside in a few minutes." She blew her nose and wiped the tears from her face, trying to repair the damage so her son wouldn't realize she had been crying.

She wearily entered their humble home. "I'm here, Son." She bent and drew him close for a hug, drawing comfort from the little arms wrapped tightly around her shoulders. "Now, tell me why you were calling for me."

His sweet little voice was tentative as he replied, "Mother, I know you said we needed to wait awhile before we eat, but I'm really hungry. I'm so hungry my stomach is hurting. Can we eat now? Please?" Each word was like a knife stabbing her in the heart. She had been so careful with their meager supply of food and now it was almost gone.

A huge boulder seemed to have settled in her throat, but she managed to reply, "You go outside and

play for a little while. We'll eat soon, but we need to wait a little longer."

She waited until he went outside and then slowly walked to the once fully stocked supply area. There was only a little meal left in the barrel and just a tiny bit of oil. The knot in her stomach tightened at the frightening prospects. She had done her best, but it seemed her best wasn't good enough.

Standing in the middle of the room she inwardly screamed, "God, where are you when I need you? Don't you care that my family will soon be hungry?"

Then as clear as if she had heard the words spoken aloud, the reply from heaven came, "I have everything under control and I'll supply your need. Just trust me."

> *"I have everything under control and I'll supply your need. Just trust me."*

A sweet, unexplainable peace settled over her. No, the food hadn't suddenly multiplied, but the assurance that God was in control of their situation made all the difference.

Walking to the door of their simple dwelling, she called for her son. "Let's go gather some wood and then I'll bake some bread for dinner."

As they neared the gate of the city, her little boy whispered, "Mother, I think that man over there asked you a question."

Turning to the man, she said, "Oh, I'm sorry. Did you ask me something?"

"Yes, ma'am," he replied. "I was wondering if you would draw me a cup of water so I can have something to drink."

"Of course. It will just take me a minute."

"Oh, and, while you are at it, would you mind bringing me a little bread when you come back?"

> "God has assured me that the meal and the oil will last."

"Sir, I don't have any bread. I have just a little meal in a barrel and a tiny bit of oil left in the container. I am out here gathering sticks and then I plan to make us some bread so we can eat it and die."

Elijah replied, "Don't be afraid. Go ahead and do what you were planning to do, but make me a little cake of bread first and then feed you and your son. God has assured me that the meal and the oil will last until he sends rain upon the earth."

That sweet peace filled her soul again and she knew that this must be what God had in mind when he told her he would supply her need. She baked a cake of bread for Elijah and then prepared food for her family. And just as God had promised, the meal and oil were sufficient for their need.

Application

UNEXPECTED CIRCUMSTANCES can happen to any of us. The widow of Zarephath and my family both experienced unexpected financial difficulties. But God had everything under control and provided for our needs.

Ask yourself:

1. How do I react to unexpected circumstances?
2. What are my fears?
3. Have I learned to turn them over to God?
4. What can I do to teach my child that he/she can trust God in every situation?
5. What can I do to help a single mother carry the burden for her family?

Dear Lord,

I'm grateful I can count on you to provide my need. Help my life to be an example that will teach my child to trust in you. When difficult times arrive, help me to turn my fears over to you, and help me to have the right attitude. Make me an encouragement to others who need a helping hand or a word of comfort.

Amen.

Reflections

U SE THIS SPACE TO RESPOND to the stories or to answer the questions.

_____

_____

_____

_____

_____

_____

_____

_____

_____

_____

_____

_____

_____

_____

_____

_____

_____

_____

_____

_____

_____

_____

_____

_____

_____

_____

_____

_____

_____

_____

_____

_____

Mothers Who Made a Difference

_____

_____

_____

_____

_____

_____

_____

_____

_____

_____

_____

_____

_____

_____

_____

_____

_____

_____

Mothers Who Made a Difference

3

Because a Mother Packed a Lunch

A Mother's Story

A LOUD RUMBLE followed by the sound of grinding brakes signaled the arrival of the school bus in the neighborhood. The young mom, Susan, called, "Hey guys, I hear the bus down the street. Grab your coats and don't forget your homework."

"Mom, where is my coat?" her oldest son yelled from his bedroom.

"It's in the closet—where it's supposed to be."

"Well, that explains it. No wonder I couldn't find it."

A little voice from just above knee level asked, "Mama, where's the permission slip for our class field trip to the zoo? Did you sign it? Cause if you didn't sign it, I won't get to go."

"It's in your book bag, honey. I put some money in

> *"Hey guys, I hear the bus down the street. Grab your coats and don't forget your homework."*

an envelope so you can buy a snack and a drink. There should be enough money to buy a snack for the elephants and giraffes, too."

She handed a lunch to each child, quickly smoothed their hair, and kissed them good-bye. Whispering a prayer for their safety, she waved to the driver and inhaled a lungful of exhaust fumes as the bus drove away.

Susan entered the house and wearily flopped into a chair. *How can I be so tired? The day has just started and I already feel like I need to go back to bed.*

Mornings were the worst. She snorted as a mental picture of June Cleaver came to mind.

Mornings were the worst. She snorted as a mental picture of June Cleaver came to mind. In television's perfect world, June's house was always spotless, mealtimes were always serene and June's appearance was always flawless—right down to her high heels, starched dress, perfect hair and the strand of pearls draped around her neck.

In contrast, Susan had begun the morning with a malfunctioning alarm clock. Jumping out of bed in panic mode, she had rushed into the children's bedrooms, "Boys, I know you're still sleepy, but you have to get up right away. The alarm didn't go off and we overslept. The bus will be here soon, so put it in gear. Get your clothes on and then come eat a bowl of cereal."

Mothers Who Made a Difference

Unlike Ward Cleaver with his calm sit-down breakfast on *Leave It to Beaver*, her husband had rushed to work without breakfast.

While the children ate cold cereal, she had assembled peanut butter sandwiches, and then added fruit, chips, and a drink to their lunch boxes.

June Cleaver she was not.

Susan noticed her next-door neighbor exiting the house, obviously on her way to work. She looked stylish and professional in her red power suit, complete with the perfect accessories, and a leather portfolio that was an exact match to her expensive black pumps. Her blonde hair was sleek and shiny and she looked every inch the up-and-coming executive climbing the corporate ladder.

In contrast, Susan was still in her pajamas and robe, each one accessorized with a smear of peanut butter from the morning's hasty lunch assembly. Her reflection in the window reminded her that she hadn't even combed her hair yet this morning. And the only ladder she'd be climbing today was the one she'd need to wash the windows in the family room.

> *Her reflection in the window reminded her that she hadn't even combed her hair yet this morning.*

She glanced around the room. No one would ever suspect she had cleaned the house only the day before.

The laundry hamper she had emptied the previous day was once again overflowing with mountains of laundry waiting to be conquered.

"God, I'm so discouraged. Sometimes I feel as if what I do as a mother is so unimportant in your eyes. My heart's desire is to do something big for you, yet I feel like I spend all my time wiping runny noses, making the beds I made just the day before, cleaning the same kitchen that I cleaned the night before, and folding the same clothes that I've folded time and time again. God, do you find any value in what I do?"

Entering the kitchen, she turned on the radio, and with God's perfect timing, this is what she heard, "Are you a mom who's discouraged today? Do you feel like your job as a mom is unimportant? Well, God thinks mothers are important and he wants you to realize that he can take anything you do and use it for his glory. Stop and think about it: Because a mother packed a lunch with five loaves and two fish, her child was part of a *miracle*."

> *"He can take anything you do and use it for his glory."*

The minister continued, "And have you ever stopped to think about the manner God chose to send his son to earth? He could have sent him in any number of ways, but when God sent his son to earth, he

sent him special delivery—by way of a mother. That's how much God values motherhood and that's how much he values you."

"God sent him special delivery—by way of a mother."

Trust God for great things; with your five loaves and two fishes, he will show you a way to feed thousands.

—Horace Bushnell

Straight from Scripture

AFTER THESE THINGS Jesus went over the Sea of Galilee, which is *the Sea* of Tiberias.

Then a great multitude followed Him, because they saw His signs which He performed on those who were diseased.

And Jesus went up on the mountain, and there He sat with His disciples.

Now the Passover, a feast of the Jews, was near.

Then Jesus lifted up *His* eyes, and seeing a great multitude coming toward Him, He said to Philip, "Where shall we buy bread, that these may eat?"

But this He said to test him, for He Himself knew what He would do.

Philip answered Him, "Two hundred denarii worth of bread is not sufficient for them, that every one of them may have a little."

One of his disciples, Andrew, Simon Peter's brother, said to Him, "There is a lad here who has five barley loaves and two small fish, but what are they among so many?"

Then Jesus said, "Make the people sit down." Now there was much grass in the place. So the men sat down, in number about five thousand.

And Jesus took the loaves, and when He had given thanks He distributed *them* to the disciples, and the disciples to those sitting down; and likewise of the fish, as much as they wanted.

So when they were filled, He said to His disciples, "Gather up the fragments that remain, so that nothing is lost."

Therefore they gathered *them* up, and filled twelve baskets with the fragments of the five barley loaves which were left over by those who had eaten. (John 6:1–13)

Mothers of the Bible

A HOT BREEZE DRIFTED through the window. The young mother felt drained—physically, emotionally, and yes, even spiritually. Reaching a tired hand to her brow, she wiped away the beads of perspiration.

Her shoulders sagged. Glancing around the house and yard, she felt overwhelmed by everything that had to be accomplished that day.

> *The young mother felt drained—physically, emotionally, and yes, even spiritually.*

She began clearing away the remains of the morning meal. Groaning in frustration, she tried to decide where to begin. *How can I be so tired? The day has just started and I already feel like I need to go back to bed.*

Noticing the lamps were almost empty, she filled them with oil, trimmed the wicks, and set them aside, ready for use when the evening shadows would appear.

The bleating of the sheep reminded her that they were waiting for their meal. She slipped her feet into leather sandals, then walked outside, gathered their food, and opened the gate into the pen. As she tossed the feed, she mentally took note of yet another chore to add to her list—the sheep would need shearing soon.

Grabbing a pail and a stool, she continued to the enclosure where the goats impatiently waited for their morning milking session. She wrinkled her nose in distaste at the pungent aroma of "fresh country air."

The pail was almost full of milk when she heard the sound of rocks scattering. As she looked up, her little boy came into view, skidding to a halt beside her. "Mother, guess what? Oh, you'll never believe it!" he cried, excitement causing him to talk so fast she could barely understand him.

"Jesus of Nazareth just came over the Sea of Galilee. He is going to be close by and we can hear him speak."

Smiling in amusement, she patted his shoulder and said, "Why don't you slow down and tell me what has you so excited."

"One of the men working in the field with Father told him that Jesus of Nazareth just came over the Sea of Galilee. They say he is going to be close by and we can hear him speak. A big crowd will be there and I really want to go. Oh, Mother, please will you go with me? Pleeease," the little lad begged, "I want you to go too."

His mother fondly tousled his hair. "Son, I'd love nothing better but you know today is my day to wash clothes. And if I don't grind the grain and make some fresh bread, you won't have anything to eat tomorrow."

His head drooped in dejection. "I know, but if I don't go today I might never again get the chance to meet Jesus. I can't believe he's here! When I was with Father near the city yesterday, everyone was telling the most amazing stories about this Jesus. One man said he heard Jesus tell a lame man at Bethesda to rise up and walk, and the man picked up his bed and walked. They said he had been lame for thirty-eight years."

> *"Everyone was telling the most amazing stories about this Jesus."*

"I've heard similar stories, Son. Last week when I went to the well to draw water, one of the other women told me she was at a wedding and Jesus turned water into wine. She wouldn't have believed it, but she actually saw it happen, and she tasted the wine."

"Oh, Mother, please can we go hear him? He might do something like that today, and we'd actually get to see it happen." He looked up at her with that pleading look that always melted her heart.

She thought a moment. "Son, I've already told you I have too much to do today, but you could go with some of the men if it's okay with them and

Father. Go to the field and find out and then come back and let me know what they say."

He threw his arms around her. "You're the best mother in the whole world." Then he ran to the field as fast as his little legs would carry him.

She smiled as she watched him. *What a dear little lad.*

It seemed only a moment before he was back. "Mother, I can go! Father said to tell you I will probably be gone quite awhile."

She grabbed a basket and lovingly filled it with five loaves and two fish.

"I'm glad you can go, honey. You will have to tell me all about it when you get home. Now, go wash your face while I pack a lunch for you."

She grabbed a basket and lovingly filled it with five loaves and two fish. *That should be plenty to feed one hungry little boy.*

She handed him his lunch and watched until he was out of sight. Then she returned to the monotony of her day, disappointment and fatigue wrapping around her like a heavy blanket.

She picked up the broom and swept the floor—the same one she had swept the day before.

She took the dirty laundry to the stream and scrubbed the clothes until they were clean—just as she had done so many times before.

While the clothes were drying in the hot sun, she

Mothers Who Made a Difference

carefully weeded around the cucumbers, garlic, and onions in the garden—exactly as she had done the day before.

She took a stone and ground the barley, combined the meal with the salt and water, then kneaded the dough until it was ready. Gathering some sticks, stubble, and dried animal dung, she stoked the fire to boil meat and to bake bread—just as she had done the day before.

Every day seemed the same—a mirror image of the boring day that preceded it.

"God, I'm so discouraged. Sometimes I feel as if what I do as a mother is so unimportant in your eyes. Is there any value in what I do?"

She wiped the tears from her eyes, then noticing the lengthening shadows, she lit the lamps she had prepared that morning. Her little lad should be home soon.

As she prepared the figs and grapes for the evening meal, she heard the familiar sound of little feet running to the house.

"Mother, you aren't going to believe what happened today!" His face was glowing as he handed her his basket. "I think everybody in town must have been there to hear Jesus. I've never seen so many people. People were crying as they listened to him. We were

> *"Sometimes I feel as if what I do as a mother is so unimportant in your eyes."*

there for hours but it seemed like we were only there for a few minutes."

"Did you actually get to see him, Son?"

"Oh, Mother, this is the really exciting part. I was standing in the crowd listening to Jesus when some of his disciples walked up to me and asked what I had in my basket. I told them you had packed me a lunch of five loaves and two fish. They told me to come with them, and they took me right to Jesus."

"Well, why did they do that, Son?"

"Jesus knew everyone was hungry. And you know what he did? He took my basket with five loaves and two fish, and he prayed over it. Then he started breaking the bread, and then the fish. There was enough to feed everyone in the crowd—and there were baskets of food left over. He did all of that with the basket you packed for me."

> *"I can take anything you do and use it for my glory."*

Then as clear as if she had heard the words spoken aloud, she heard God say, "I can take anything you do and use it for my glory—no matter how small and insignificant it seems to you. Because you were faithful in the little things—because you packed a lunch with five loaves and two fish—I was able to use your child as part of a *miracle. That's* the value of a mother."

Application

THE RESPONSIBILITIES of motherhood can often be exhausting and are sometimes overwhelming. Susan and the young lad's mom loved their children and loved being moms, but they sometimes felt that what they were doing was unimportant in God's eyes.

Ask yourself:

1. Do I sometimes feel unimportant in God's eyes?
2. How can God use my daily tasks as a mom for his glory?
3. How do I handle discouragement? Do I wallow in it or do I go to God and ask for his help?
4. Do I understand now that God values moms?

Dear Lord,

Please help me to be faithful in the little things. Help me to be a godly example to my child and give me wisdom as I raise this child for you. Give me a sweet attitude as I go about my daily tasks and help me to remember that you value my job as a mom. Thank you for being with me every step of the way. *Amen.*

Reflections

USE THIS SPACE TO RESPOND to the stories or to answer the questions.

_____

_____

_____

_____

_____

_____

_____

_____

_____

_____

_____

_____

_____

_____

_____

_____

_____

_____

_____

_____

_____

_____

_____

_____

_____

_____

_____

_____

_____

_____

_____

_____

_____

Mothers Who Made a Difference

4

Because a Mother Prayed a Prayer

A Mother's Story

HOW CAN THIS NEWS be so happy and exciting yet rip my heart into shreds at the same time?

Their daughters and sons-in-law had gathered at Bill and Ruth's house for dinner. Now that Karen and Samantha were married, evenings with the entire family at the dinner table were cherished events.

As they enjoyed dessert, Karen said, "Andy and I want to tell you something while we're all here. God is calling us to the mission field. We've prayed about this for a long time and he's given us peace about it. We'll be moving to Costa Rica to attend language school and to help with some of their ministries."

> *"God is calling us to the mission field."*

Everyone began talking at once—which was a

good thing, because Ruth couldn't have said a word if her life had depended on it.

She was thrilled. Really. Ruth's one desire had always been for her children to serve God. But this was her baby girl. Okay, so Karen happened to be twenty-five years old. But that didn't make her any less precious to Ruth, and Costa Rica was so far away.

> *Ruth's one desire had always been for her children to serve God.*

The evening zoomed by as Karen and Andy shared their plans. As she hugged Karen good-bye, Ruth squeezed her close for a long moment. "I'm proud of you." Emotion clogged her throat. "I can't think of anything I want more than to have you serve God."

Bill and Ruth waved as everyone packed into their cars and left. Bill put his arm around Ruth. "It's been an emotional evening, hasn't it?"

She gave him a wry smile. "I'd call it the happiest sad evening of my life."

Both of them were lost in their own thoughts as they prepared for bed. For Ruth, the hours ticked by in the darkened room, her mind whirling with memories.

They had been so excited the day Karen was born. She was such a beautiful baby. She remembered the day they had stood in church and dedicated her to the Lord. Their pastor had held the sweet baby girl in his arms and prayed, "God, we

thank you for loaning Karen to Bill and Ruth. We ask you to guide her life. Help her to accept you as her Savior when she's old enough to understand. Protect and watch over her. Touch her life and give her a willing heart to serve you. Amen."

Ruth had stood there that day and silently prayed, *God, please help me to be a good mother. Thank you for the gift of this child. I realize she's only on loan to us. Whatever it takes, I want your will for her life.*

With that memory frozen in her mind, Ruth knelt beside her bed. "Lord, you blessed my life with this precious daughter. She's been one of my most priceless gifts. Now I'm loaning her back to you. Please give me the grace to bear it when she leaves for Costa Rica. Amen."

The next few months flew by as they helped Karen and Andy prepare for the move.

It was during the quiet hours of the night when Ruth's fears surfaced. What will happen if they get sick? Will the healthcare be adequate? What about the parasites and disease-carrying bugs they'll encounter? Where will they live? Will they be safe? Her mind whirled with scary possibilities.

Then the thought dawned on her: *The God who*

God, please help me to be a good mother. Thank you for the gift of this child.

took care of her daughter when she was at home—the God who had taken care of Karen since the day she was born—was the same God who would take care of her in Costa Rica. A sweet peace swept over her.

Soon the time arrived for Karen and Andy to begin their adventure at language school.

Being apart was tough on all of them, but God was using Karen and Andy to touch hearts and lives.

Months later, Bill and Ruth visited them in Costa Rica. As they left customs, excited cries of "Mama! Daddy!" filled the air. *Oh, how wonderful to see their precious faces again.*

God would take care of her in Costa Rica.

Ruth looked out the window in fascination while they drove through the neighborhoods of San Jose. "Lord, keep them safe on these roads," she prayed, observing the anything-goes traffic with horns blowing, cars darting in and out in a crazy manner, and bicyclists riding in the middle of the chaos.

Over the next few days, cultural differences became apparent when they saw houses surrounded by tall walls topped with barbed wire and as they ate beans and rice at every meal. They enjoyed the lush beauty of the rain forest, visited a coffee plantation, and witnessed the Arenal Volcano erupt against the background of the night sky.

  *Mothers Who Made a Difference*

But the highlight of the trip was seeing God use Karen and Andy to minister to the Costa Rican people.

Ruth watched with emotion as Karen walked through the nursing home, dispensing hugs and smiles to the residents in their wheelchairs. Andy presented the gospel in Spanish, and nine precious souls invited Jesus into their hearts.

Tears misted her eyes as she watched Karen perform a Bible story puppet show at an orphanage. *I'll always remember the image of my daughter loving on those sweet children who have no mother or daddy to dry their tears or kiss their bruised knees.*

Ruth wiped tears from her cheeks as they entered a poverty-stricken neighborhood. *Forgive me for taking so much for granted, Lord.* The dirt-floored shacks were patched together wooden pallets and scraps of metal. Gaping holes in the walls allowed water to flood in when it rained. Ruth's heart shattered as she watched children with no shoes walk through the sewage-contaminated soil.

Forgive me for taking so much for granted, Lord.

As Karen exited the vehicle, children ran to her, smiles on their faces. "Señora Karen!" Ruth watched her daughter scoop them into her arms, laughing and speaking to them in Spanish. *This is where she's meant to be—in the middle of Costa Rica—and in the middle of God's will.*

She watched Andy and Karen visit each tiny shack sharing their love and God's message of salvation. *Thank you for letting me see this, Lord. Thank you for answering the prayer I prayed so many years ago when I dedicated Karen to you. She really was only on loan to me.*

Now she belongs to you.

> *Lord, you blessed my life with this precious child. Now I'm loaning her back to you.*

Children are the living messages
we send to a time we will not see.
—John W. Whitehead

Straight from Scripture

NOW THERE WAS a certain man ... and his name *was* Elkanah....

And he had two wives: the name of one *was* Hannah, and the name of the other Peninnah. Peninnah had children, but Hannah had no children.

This man went up from his city yearly to worship and sacrifice to the LORD of hosts in Shiloh. Also the two sons of Eli, Hophni and Phinehas, the priests of the LORD, *were* there.

And whenever the time came for Elkanah to make an offering, he would give portions to Peninnah his wife and to all her sons and daughters.

But to Hannah he would give a double portion, for he loved Hannah, although the LORD had closed her womb.

And her rival also provoked her severely, to make her miserable, because the LORD had closed her womb.

So it was, year by year, when she went up to the

house of the LORD, that she provoked her; therefore she wept and did not eat.

Then Elkanah her husband said to her, "Hannah, why do you weep? Why do you not eat? And why is your heart grieved? *Am* I not better to you than ten sons?"

So Hannah arose after they had finished eating and drinking in Shiloh. Now Eli the priest was sitting on the seat by the doorpost of the tabernacle of the LORD.

And she *was* in bitterness of soul, and prayed to the LORD and wept in anguish.

Then she made a vow and said, "O LORD of hosts, if You will indeed look on the affliction of Your maidservant and remember me, and not forget Your maidservant, but will give Your maidservant a male child, then I will give him to the LORD all the days of his life, and no razor shall come upon his head."

And it happened, as she continued praying before the LORD, that Eli watched her mouth.

Now Hannah spoke in her heart; only her lips moved, but her voice was not heard. Therefore Eli thought she was drunk.

So Eli said to her, "How long will you be drunk? Put your wine away from you!"

But Hannah answered and said, "No, my lord, I *am* a woman of sorrowful spirit. I have drunk neither wine nor intoxicating drink, but have poured out my soul before the LORD." …

  *Mothers Who Made a Difference*

Then Eli answered and said, "Go in peace, and the God of Israel grant your petition which you have asked of Him." ...

So it came to pass in the process of time that Hannah conceived and bore a son, and called his name Samuel, *saying*, "Because I have asked for him from the LORD."

Now the man Elkanah and all his house went up to offer to the LORD the yearly sacrifice and his vow.

But Hannah did not go up, for she said to her husband, "*Not* until the child is weaned; then I will take him, that he may appear before the LORD and remain there forever." ...

Now when she had weaned him, she took him up with her, with three bulls, one ephah of flour, and a skin of wine, and brought him to the house of the LORD in Shiloh. And the child *was* young....

And she said, "O my lord! As your soul lives, my lord, I *am* the woman who stood by you here, praying to the LORD.

"For this child I prayed, and the LORD has granted me my petition which I asked of Him.

"Therefore I also have lent him to the LORD; as long as he lives he shall be lent to the LORD." So they worshiped the LORD there....

But Samuel ministered before the LORD, *even as* a child, wearing a linen ephod.

Moreover his mother used to make him a little

 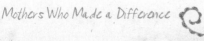 

robe, and bring *it* to him year by year when she came up with her husband to offer the yearly sacrifice.…

And the child Samuel grew in stature, and in favor both with the LORD and men.

(1 Sam. 1:1–15, 17, 20–22, 24, 26–28; 2:18–19, 26)

Mothers Who Made a Difference

Mothers of the Bible

*P*ENINNAH'S CRUEL WORDS hit their intended target with the force of a physical blow, inflicting barbed wounds in Hannah's tender soul. "Well, Hannah, another year has arrived, and you still don't have a child to take to the temple. Elkanah is excited about taking our newest baby for his first visit this year." She smiled spitefully. "I think he loves me more with every child I give him. You must have done something really bad for God to shut your womb and make you barren."

> *"You must have done something really bad for God to shut your womb and make you barren."*

Hannah turned away, determined not to let Peninnah see the naked pain on her face. The word "barren" seemed to hang in the air, a haunting reminder that mocked Hannah. When she was alone, she cried until there were no more tears left in her.

She was so tired of Peninnah's caustic comments. Even more, she was tired of being barren. Her arms and heart ached for a child to fill them—but they were empty.

Elkanah's voice drifted in from outside. "Hannah, it's time to leave for the temple. Are you ready?"

"I'll be right there."

Excited greetings from distant friends and family filled the air as they arrived in the city. Hannah tugged at Elkanah's cloak sleeve. "You stay here and visit. I'll meet you back here. I want to pray at the temple for a little while. I shouldn't be too long."

An awareness of God's presence filled her soul.

As Hannah entered the temple, an awareness of God's presence filled her soul. She dropped to her knees and focused on the purpose of her visit. Her lips moved silently, "God, I'm here today, begging you one more time to give me a child. You know I want a child more than anything." Spasms of tears shook her. "If you'll give me a son, I promise I'll give him back to you, to serve you all the days of his life."

Eli, the priest, bent down and touched Hannah on the shoulder. "I've been watching you. Your behavior has been a little unusual since you entered the temple. I've noticed your lips moving, but you aren't saying anything. Are you drunk?"

"Oh, no sir, I'm not drunk. I'm a woman with a broken heart pleading with God to answer my prayer."

Hannah's faith touched him, and he responded, "God will answer the prayer you prayed today."

She ran through the streets of the city, happy tears trickling down her cheeks. She couldn't wait to tell her husband.

"Elkanah, you aren't going to believe what happened! I was praying in the temple, crying and begging God to give me a child. I promised God that if he would give me a son, I would give the child back to serve him. Eli, the priest, came and talked to me. He said that God will answer my prayer. I'm so excited."

Time went by, and the day Hannah had dreamed about arrived. She was finally able to tell her husband, "We're going to have a baby!"

She enjoyed every phase of her pregnancy, each new experience even more precious because she once thought she would never become a mother.

Then the joyous day arrived when her son was born. She was instantly smitten, her heart captured by the tiny babe cuddled in her arms.

> "God will answer the prayer you prayed today."

"What should we name him, Hannah?" the proud father asked.

"Samuel would be the perfect name since I asked the Lord for him."

"I agree. Samuel it is, then."

The months passed, and Hannah blossomed in her role as mother. Each new stage in Samuel's life brought joy and excitement.

"Elkanah, look, he's learned to roll over."

He winked at her. "He's brilliant—just like his father."

Months later, they celebrated Samuel's latest achievement as he learned to crawl.

> *"Samuel would be the perfect name since I asked the Lord for him."*

Hannah had never been happier. She spent long hours cuddling her son, stroking his soft baby skin, and kissing his chubby feet. "Samuel, I'm so glad the Lord loaned you to me. I love you, little one."

The time arrived for the family's yearly trip to the temple. Hannah told Elkanah, "I'm not going to go this year. Once Samuel is weaned, I'll go with you, and I'll leave him at the temple to serve the Lord, just like I promised."

The months passed and Hannah knew her time with her son would soon be over. She spent every moment she could with her precious little boy, capturing each memory and storing it in her heart for the days when he would no longer be with her.

  *Mothers Who Made a Difference*

As the weeks began counting down to the yearly temple visit, Hannah struggled with the whirling emotions inside her. *God, I meant that prayer I prayed at the temple that day. I'm going to loan Samuel back to you like I promised. I just didn't know it would be this hard to give him up. I didn't know how much I'd miss him. I didn't know the overwhelming love I'd feel for this child.*

> *I didn't know the overwhelming love I'd feel for this child.*

Her fears began to surface. *What if Samuel gets hurt or becomes sick? Will Eli take good care of him? He's just a little boy. How will I survive without him?* Her mind whirled with scary possibilities.

Then the thought dawned on her: *The God who took care of her son when he was at home—the God who had taken care of Samuel since the day he was born—was the same God who would take care of him at the temple.* A sweet peace swept over her.

The time arrived for their yearly trip. Elkanah and Hannah were both quiet as they traveled, each lost in their own thoughts.

Hannah entered the temple, holding her precious little boy. She remembered her last visit and her desperation as she had begged God for a child. Now here she was, carrying the answer to that prayer in her arms. And now the time had arrived

for her to honor the commitment she had made that day.

She was thrilled. Really. She had always wanted her son to serve God, but Samuel had become so precious to her. *I don't know how I'll bear it without him.*

Holding Samuel in her arms, she knelt in the same spot where she had prayed before. "Lord, you blessed my life with this precious child. He's been one of my most priceless gifts." She wiped the tears from her cheeks. "Now I'm loaning him back to you. Please give me the grace to bear it when I leave him at the temple. Amen."

She noticed Eli, the priest, across the place of worship. "Sir, do you remember me? I'm the woman who was here praying for God to send me a child. You told me that God would answer my prayer." She kissed Samuel's soft cheek. "This is my son—God's gift to me. Now I'm loaning him back to God so he can serve him all the days of his life."

> *"This is my son—God's gift to me."*

Tears blinded Hannah's eyes as she left the temple, her arms empty once again. This was the happiest sad day of her life.

Their home felt empty when Hannah and Elkanah returned from the trip. The thick silence was deafening. How she missed Samuel's sweet voice

and the sound of his little feet running through the house.

The months dragged by, and soon it was time for the family to travel to the temple once again. Hannah was so excited about seeing her son. She had made him a little robe, a mother's love woven in with each tiny stitch.

She noticed Samuel immediately when they arrived. *Oh, how wonderful to see his precious face again.* With tears in her eyes, she stood and watched as Samuel performed his tasks at the temple. God was using her son to serve him. *This is where he's meant to be—in the middle of the temple—and in the middle of God's will.*

> *God was using her son to serve him.*

Thank you for letting me see this, Lord. He really was only on loan to me.

Now he belongs to you.

Application

RUTH AND HANNAH learned that their children were only on loan from God. Despite their sincere desire for their child to serve God, each of them struggled with their fears and emotional pain.

Ask yourself:

1. Have I dedicated my child to the Lord?
2. Have I realized that my child is only on loan to me?
3. Am I willing to let go of my child for his service?
4. Do I pray faithfully that my child will follow God's will for his/her life?

Dear heavenly Father,

Thank you for the priceless gift of my child. I realize that this child is only on loan to me, and I give him/her back to you for your service. When the time arrives, help my child to be obedient to your leading and to stay in the center of your will. Help me to be faithful in my role as mom.

Amen.

Reflections

*U*SE THIS SPACE TO RESPOND to the stories or to answer the questions.

_____
_____
_____
_____
_____
_____
_____
_____
_____
_____
_____
_____
_____

_____

_____

_____

_____

_____

_____

_____

_____

_____

_____

_____

_____

_____

_____

_____

_____

_____

_____

Mothers Who Made a Difference

5

Because a
Mother
Misplaced
a
Son

A Mother's Story

MICHAEL, MY SON, *is going to stand and preach on the same mountain where Jesus once preached.* Lorraine pinched herself to see if the moment was real.

I want to remember every detail of this day. She gazed at the distant mountains and the Sea of Galilee visible from the Mount of Beatitudes. A gentle breeze carried the aroma of the flowering trees across the mountaintop.

The tour of the Holy Land was a dream come true for Lorraine and she couldn't think of anything more wonderful than sharing the experience with her son as

> *A gentle breeze carried the aroma of the flowering trees across the mountaintop.*

the pages of the Bible literally came to life before their eyes. Their trip to Israel had already been amazing, but this day would be one she would cherish forever.

Precious memories of Michael as a child filtered through her mind while she waited for the service to begin. He had been the sweetest little boy, and from the day he was born, he had filled their home with sunshine and laughter. He had never been rebellious, had never given them any problems or caused them to worry—well, except for that one time. Her smile faded as she remembered the day three-year-old Michael had disappeared.

> *Precious memories of Michael as a child filtered through her mind.*

"Doug, I can't find Michael. He isn't in the house or the yard. I've looked everywhere." Panic filled her as she called her husband. *Where could Michael be? Did someone kidnap him? Did he wander into the woods?*

"I'll be there in a few minutes, honey. Look through the house one more time in case he might be playing hide-and-seek, and then call the neighbors. Try not to worry. I'm sure we'll find him." Doug tried to sound reassuring even though his own heart felt like it was about to jump out of his chest.

The minutes had seemed like days as they searched for him.

"Doug, what if he's lost in the woods? It's supposed to be cold tonight. He could freeze to death. And I know there are wild animals. I saw a fox

  *Mothers Who Made a Difference*

and a bobcat just last week. He's just a little boy. What will he do if one of those animals comes after him?"

"Honey, I'm sure we'll find him before it gets dark. Just keep praying and keep calling his name."

The relief was overwhelming when they finally found him playing on the swings in a neighbor's yard.

Lorraine had often felt inadequate as a mom. However, on those occasions, God usually reminded her of the words from a special sermon her pastor had preached on Mother's Day when Michael was just a baby. "All God requires from you is a willing heart. Then you can count on him to be there every step of the way and to supply all the skills you need to be a good mother."

Her mind drifted to happier times as she remembered the day six-year-old Michael invited Jesus into his heart. He went to his Sunday school class the next morning and asked the teacher if he could speak to the class.

> *"Just keep praying and keep calling his name."*

"Something special happened to me yesterday. I asked Jesus to come into my heart. Some of you might not know how to do that so I want to tell you all about it. This is what you need to do if you want to ask him into your heart. First, you have to understand that you've done bad things and that makes Jesus sad. I lied to my mama and I stole some cookies one time. That's called sin.

"God says that the price for sin is death. Jesus died on the cross so that we wouldn't have to die for our sins. My mama prayed with me and I asked Jesus to forgive me and to come into my heart. You can do that, too."

Lorraine had wondered if he might someday become an evangelist. *Now, here I am, watching my dreams for my son come true.*

> *"Have you ever just sat and thought about how much God has blessed you?"*

Michael's voice carried across the mountain as he read Matthew 5:3–4, "Blessed are the poor in spirit, for theirs is the kingdom of heaven. Blessed are those who mourn, for they shall be comforted." He finished reading the familiar chapter and then he began his sermon. "Have you ever just sat and thought about how much God has blessed you?"

Lorraine sat there, a mother's love and pride flooding through her. *That's my son they're listening to with such rapt attention. He speaks with such authority.* She'd never seen this side of him before. Then the realization hit her once again that the son she loved so much was no longer her little boy. A man now stood in his place—God's man.

  *Mothers Who Made a Difference*

The child I once cradled in my arms is now God's messenger of salvation. With awe, Lorraine bowed her head and thanked God once again for blessing her with the most special job on earth—being a mother.

The child I once cradled in my arms is now God's messenger of salvation.

If God gave his own Son for us, how could he ever bring himself to desert us in small things?
—Martin Luther

Straight from Scripture

A ND THE CHILD GREW and became strong in spirit, filled with wisdom; and the grace of God was upon him.

His parents went to Jerusalem every year at the Feast of the Passover.

And when He was twelve years old, they went up to Jerusalem according to the custom of the feast.

When they had finished the days, as they returned, the Boy Jesus lingered behind in Jerusalem. And Joseph and His mother did not know *it*; but supposing Him to have been in the company, they went a day's journey, and sought Him among *their* relatives and acquaintances.

So when they did not find Him, they returned to Jerusalem, seeking Him.

Now so it was *that* after three days they found Him in the temple, sitting in the midst of the teachers, both listening to them and asking them questions.

And all who heard Him were astonished at His understanding and answers.

So when they saw Him, they were amazed; and His mother said to Him, "Son, why have You done this to us? Look, Your father and I have sought You anxiously."

And He said to them, "Why did you seek Me? Did you not know that I must be about My Father's business?"

But they did not understand the statement which He spoke to them.

Then He went down with them and came to Nazareth, and was subject to them, but His mother kept all these things in her heart.

And Jesus increased in wisdom and stature, and in favor with God and men. (Luke 2:40–52)

Mothers Who Made a Difference

Mothers of the Bible

HYSTERIA TINGED MARY'S voice as she cried, "God trusted me with his son—and I've lost him! Joseph, what am I going to do? We have to find him!" Tears poured down her cheeks leaving a trail in the gritty sand particles imbedded in her face. "Oh dear, I've *lost* God's Son!"

Joseph squeezed her hand reassuringly, "Calm down, we'll find him. Jesus is probably somewhere on the road with our friends or the rest of the family. Why, look at all the multitudes of people traveling home from Jerusalem today. We're probably just having trouble spotting him in the crowd."

> *"God trusted me with his son—and I've lost him!"*

"But what if we don't find him? Joseph, what if something bad has happened to him?" Panic lined her face. "Don't you remember how Herod wanted to kill him when he was young and we had to escape during the night and go into hiding? What if someone else wants to do him harm? We haven't seen him all day. *Anything* could have happened to him."

She wrung her hands in despair. "The day the angel first came to tell me about Jesus, I told him this job was too big for me. I told him I was too young and I didn't know anything about being a mother, much less being a mother to God's Son."

"I didn't know anything about being a mother, much less being a mother to God's Son."

"Mary, look at me. Don't you remember the wise advice the angel gave you that day? All God requires from you is a willing heart. Then you can count on him to be there every step of the way and to supply all the skills you need to be a good mother. Everything will be fine. Let's turn around and head back to Jerusalem. You take the right side of the road and I'll take the left side, and we'll ask everyone we pass if they've seen Jesus. We'll find him in a little while. I'm sure he's back there somewhere."

The trip had been wonderful up to this point. Along with family and friends, they had left home days earlier and traveled to Jerusalem to celebrate the Feast of the Passover. This was always such a special

Mothers Who Made a Difference

time as they worshipped together as a family and remembered God's faithfulness in delivering the children of Israel from Pharaoh's control. How could things have gone from wonderful to bad so quickly?

The frantic search began. Mary darted through the crowd, "Please, can you help me? I can't find my son. His name is Jesus and he's twelve years old. Have you seen him?"

Noticing a familiar face in the crowd, Joseph ran over and asked, "Have you seen Jesus? We thought he was with our friends or other family members, and now we can't find him. Please, if you see Jesus, tell him we're looking for him and we're sick with worry."

They asked the same questions repeatedly, and when night fell, they still hadn't found their son. Exhausted, Mary finally fell into a fitful sleep, jarring awake every few hours to ask, "Is he here? Did you find Jesus?"

The search resumed the next morning with renewed hope. "I'm sure we'll find him today, Mary." But many long, hot hours later, the day ended in discouragement with Jesus still missing.

"Please, if you see Jesus, tell him we're looking for him."

By day four of their search, hope was dwindling, and Mary and Joseph looked as if they had aged ten years. They were exhausted, their eyes were red-rimmed, and their feet were raw from the long days of searching and the constant friction of sand and pebbles inside their sandals.

"We're not going to find Jesus," Mary whispered in defeat.

Joseph wrapped her in his arms, "Mary, we won't give up. We'll keep searching until we find him. We're almost to the city now. We'll go from house to house and down every alleyway if we have to, but we won't give up until we find him. God knows where Jesus is and he will show us."

> *"God knows where Jesus is and he will show us."*

As they approached the city market, the aroma of hot food mingled with the sounds of merchants selling their wares. Fresh hope filled Mary's eyes. "Joseph, maybe Jesus is here in the market. This would have to be exciting for a young boy to see all the activity and the food and the shops. He might be in one of the inns or watching one of the merchants weaving or making pottery."

"That's probably where he is, Mary. I'll take this side and you take the other side of the market. We'll keep asking. I'm sure someone has seen him."

"Please, I'm looking for my twelve-year-old son. His name is Jesus. Have you seen him?"

"Have you seen a young lad at the market the

last few days? He is missing and we are so worried. His name is Jesus."

They repeated the questions in all the shops, their optimism fading as they reached the end of the market.

Glancing upward, Joseph noticed the temple at the top of the hill. "Mary, the last place we were with Jesus was at the temple. He's probably looking for us, too. Maybe he's waiting there for us. Wouldn't that make sense to a young lad?"

"Come on, honey. Let's go inside and see what he's doing in the temple."

As they neared the doors of the temple, Mary came to an abrupt halt. "Joseph, I must be hearing things. I thought I heard Jesus talking inside the temple."

Joseph listened intently, and then a slow smile spread across his tired face. "Mary, you're not hearing things. I hear him too!" He caught her in his arms as the sudden relief from the worry and tension caused her knees to buckle. The bottled-up tears came streaming out and he stroked her hair with tender hands until the tide of emotion was past, his tears of relief joining hers.

"Come on, honey. Let's go inside and see what he's doing in the temple."

They slipped quietly inside the doors and then

looked at each other in stunned disbelief. Mary whispered, "Joseph, Jesus is talking to the priests in the temple. Why, he's just a boy, and yet they're listening to his every word as if he were their equal. Listen to the questions they're asking him."

"Jesus, what do you think a man must do to enter the kingdom of heaven? I've been faithful in giving sacrifices and praying daily in the synagogue. I've honored my father and my mother. I've been good to my neighbor. Don't you think that will be enough to please Jehovah God?"

"What do you think is the most important commandment?"

"How are we to know the truth when there are so many false prophets?"

"What do you mean when you say the Messiah is come?"

The priests were astounded as Jesus replied to their questions with wisdom and certainty, and they responded with respect as Jesus asked questions of them.

Mary stood there, a mother's love and pride flooding through her. *That's my son they're listening to with such rapt attention.* The realization hit her that the son she loved so much was no longer her little boy. A man now stood in his place—God's man.

The priests were astounded as Jesus replied to their questions with wisdom and certainty.

Mothers Who Made a Difference

She had always known in her head that he was the Son of God, but it had never seemed real to her before that day. *He speaks with such authority.* Heaven-sent goose bumps dotted her skin as it hit her full-force: *All those years ago, when I cradled my baby boy … I held the* salvation of the world *in my arms.*"

Awe filled her being as she soaked in that special moment. Despite all her shortcomings as a mother, despite all her fears, God had been able to use the simple gift of her willing heart. And as he had promised, God had supplied her with all the skills she needed to be the mother that he had asked her to be.

With tears dripping between her fingers, Mary bowed her head and thanked God for granting her the joy and the privilege of the most special job on earth—being a mother.

> *God had supplied her with all the skills she needed to be the mother that he had asked her to be.*

Application

LORRAINE AND MARY experienced times when they felt inadequate as a mother. And both of them saw the results of being a faithful mother as God used their children in a special way.

Ask yourself:

1. What should I do on those occasions when I feel inadequate as a mother?
2. Do I have a willing heart to do whatever God asks of me?
3. What are my spiritual goals for my child?
4. Have I thanked God lately for the privilege of being a mom?

Dear Lord,

There are so many times when I feel inadequate as a mom. Help me to remember that you are strong where I am weak. I bring you a willing heart and a desire to be the mother that you want me to become. Thank you for being with me whenever I am afraid. Thank you for the peace of knowing that you are always with my child. *Amen.*

Reflections

USE THIS SPACE TO RESPOND to the stories or to answer the questions.

_____
_____
_____
_____
_____
_____
_____
_____
_____
_____
_____
_____
_____

Mothers Who Made a Difference

6

Because a Mother Took a Cruise

A Mother's Story

J CAN'T BELIEVE *I'm in jail.* Ricky looked around at the other late-night residents of the drunk tank. He had been nursing his first beer when the officers arrested him, so he was sober enough to be keenly aware of his surroundings. *I hope my buddies bail me out soon.* The stench of sickness and unwashed flesh made him nauseous. Curses and rantings from the other prisoners flayed on his already strained nerves. The hours in the cell passed slowly, giving him plenty of time to think.

Ricky and his college buddies had driven to Myrtle Beach for the Easter weekend. The group was partying on the roadside with open containers of beer when the officers approached. "Pour out the drinks, boys."

> *The hours in the cell passed slowly, giving him plenty of time to think.*

The request made Ricky mad, and he walked off still holding his can of beer. Three of the officers followed. When he shoved one of them, they arrested him.

In the squad car, Ricky asked, "Why was I the only one arrested when eight of us had beers?"

"You're our example. By arresting you, your friends will think twice before drinking again."

His childhood had been picture-perfect and filled with happy memories.

That night in the humid jail cell, the words haunted him. *You're our example.* He snorted in shamed disgust. *Fine example I am. My mama would be so disappointed if she knew. I wouldn't be sitting here now if I had listened to her.*

His thoughts drifted to the comfort of home. Ruby and Earl had been wonderful parents. They had taken Ricky to church from the time he was a baby. His childhood had been picture-perfect and filled with happy memories. Every evening, the family had gathered for prayer and his mama had told exciting Bible stories about Paul and Silas, Daniel and the lion's den, and Noah and the ark.

The story about Noah had been his favorite, his little-boy mind visualizing the exotic animals walking two by two into the ark. He could probably repeat the story word for word. Closing his eyes, he

could almost hear his mother's voice as she began the story, "And God saw that the wickedness of man was great in the earth ..."

Wickedness. The word hit him with a forceful blow. *I guess I fit that description now. Paul and Silas were in jail for preaching the gospel ... and here I sit in a jail cell for drinking and living wrong.* Shamed tears misted his eyes.

His mind walked him through the downward spiral of his college years. It began when he quit going to church and chose the wrong group of friends.

The drinking came first; then the group moved on to hard liquor and marijuana. Violence walked hand in hand with the booze and drugs, and it was a common occurrence for the group to have guns and knives drawn on them.

He was relieved when his buddies arrived to bail him out of jail.

Several days later, Ricky sat in his mama's kitchen as if everything were normal, the details of his weekend a well-kept secret.

Ruby placed a piece of pie on the table. "Son, I wanted to ask you about something. Did anything happen over the weekend while you were at Myrtle Beach?"

Ricky froze, his mind frantically trying to figure out who would have called and told her. Shame filled

> *Wickedness. The word hit him with a forceful blow.*

him and he lied, "No, Mama. Everything was fine. Why?"

"Well, I woke up in the middle of the night on Saturday with a bad feeling that something had happened to you. I got out of bed and prayed for you. Are you sure nothing happened?"

Ricky was dying inside, but he kept his expression normal as he lied again, "No, Mama. Everything was fine."

"I don't understand it, then. It was one of the heaviest burdens I've ever had for you, Ricky. I stayed on my knees for a long time and begged God to take care of you." She patted him on the shoulder as she walked by, "I'm glad you're okay. Maybe God will explain to me someday why he put that burden on my heart."

> *"Maybe God will explain to me someday why he put that burden on my heart."*

Oh, Mama, if you only knew! Once again, the words "the wickedness of men" from that Bible story popped into his mind. Guilt overwhelmed him—but not enough to make him change his ways.

Ruby watched Ricky's car disappear down the driveway as he left for college. She couldn't shake the feeling that something wasn't right with her son. She'd prayed more for him the last few months than she had in his entire life.

Mothers Who Made a Difference

She walked down the hall to Ricky's bedroom and knelt beside his bed. "God, I'm here again praying for my boy. I don't know what's going on in his life, but you do. Keep him safe. You know I've always felt you had something special for him to do. Don't let him ruin his life. Touch his heart and bring him back to you." She wiped the tears from her cheeks. "In your Word, you promised that if we'd train our children to serve you that they wouldn't depart from that when they're old. I thank you that we can count on your promises—even when we don't understand the circumstances. Amen."

Ricky continued his wild lifestyle but God was dealing with his heart. His Uncle Bobby, a Baptist preacher, called him one night. "Ricky, some of my young men are leaving for college soon and I want you to talk to them about what they will face when they get there."

> "God, I'm here again praying for my boy. I don't know what's going on in his life, but you do."

Ricky tried to say no, but Bobby insisted. He knew Ricky wasn't living right, and God had impressed him to call his nephew with the request. Guilt overwhelmed Ricky. How could he go talk to those guys when his own life was such a mess?

With tears on his cheeks, he got down on his knees. "God, I know I've done wrong and I've failed

> "Never doubt the effectiveness of a mother's prayers."

you. Please forgive me. I give my life back to you. Amen."

Several years later, Ricky stood in front of the church and preached his first sermon. "My life was a mess. Then God convicted my heart and extended his love and forgiveness to me."

Tears streamed down Ruby's cheeks as Ricky told of his arrest at Myrtle Beach. Now she understood the burden God had placed on her heart to pray for her son.

Emotion colored Ricky's voice as he stood in the pulpit. "Never doubt the effectiveness of a mother's prayers. I know I'm here today because my mother prayed for me."

Behind every work of God you will always find some kneeling form.

—Dwight L. Moody

Straight from Scripture

*T*HEN THE LORD SAW that the wickedness of man *was* great in the earth, and *that* every intent of the thoughts of his heart *was* only evil continually....

So the LORD said, "I will destroy man whom I have created from the face of the earth, both man and beast, creeping thing and birds of the air, for I am sorry that I have made them."

But Noah found grace in the eyes of the LORD....

And God said to Noah, "The end of all flesh has come before Me, for the earth is filled with violence through them; and behold, I will destroy them with the earth.

"Make yourself an ark of gopherwood; make rooms in the ark, and cover it inside and outside with pitch.

"And this is how you shall make it: The length of the ark *shall* be three hundred cubits, its width fifty cubits, and its height thirty cubits.

"You shall make a window for the ark, and you

shall finish it to a cubit from above; and set the door of the ark in its side. You shall make it *with* lower, second, and third *decks*.

"And behold, I Myself am bringing floodwaters on the earth, to destroy from under heaven all flesh in which *is* the breath of life; everything that *is* on the earth shall die.

"But I will establish My covenant with you; and you shall go into the ark—you, your sons, your wife, and your sons' wives with you.

"And of every living thing of all flesh you shall bring two of every *sort* into the ark, to keep *them* alive with you; they shall be male and female.

"Of the birds after their kind, of animals after their kind, and of every creeping thing of the earth after its kind, two of every *kind* will come to you to keep *them* alive.

"And you shall take for yourself of all food that is eaten, and you shall gather *it* to yourself; and it shall be food for you and for them." …

So Noah, with his sons, his wife, and his sons' wives, went into the ark because of the waters of the flood.… And the rain was on the earth forty days and forty nights.…

So He destroyed all living things which were on the face of the ground: both man and cattle, creeping thing and bird of the air. They were destroyed from the earth. Only Noah and those who *were* with him in the ark remained *alive*. (Gen. 6:5, 7–8, 13–21; 7:7, 12, 23)

Mothers Who Made a Difference

Mothers of the Bible

"U M ... NOAH, HONEY, you've always been a pack rat, but the last few weeks things seem to be getting out of hand. The piles of gopherwood you've brought home are starting to look like mountains. What are you planning to do with all that wood?"

"I do have a purpose for it. I had planned to have a long talk with you about the situation after our evening meal."

"Noah, you sound like this is something serious."

"This is about as serious as it gets. We'll talk tonight."

Something big was about to happen. She could feel it.

The afternoon walked by on slow feet as Mrs. Noah's imagination conjured up all kinds of possibilities. The suspense was almost more than she could bear. Something big was about to happen. She could feel it.

She'd been married to Noah for a long time and she'd never heard that somber tone in his voice before.

When the meal was finally completed, the couple sat down to talk. Mrs. Noah was surprised at how nervous she felt. "Go ahead, Noah. I can sense something major is about to happen."

"Dear, God has been speaking to me. He is so grieved by the sin and wickedness of man that he is sorry he even created us."

> *"God is planning to send floodwaters and everything on earth will die."*

"I'm sure God's heart must be saddened, Noah. The two of us have talked before about how wicked things have become in our town. No one cares about serving God. All they think about is doing evil. I'm saddened too."

"Honey, God is so grieved that he is planning to destroy man and beast, creeping things, and the birds of the air from off the face of the earth."

Fear and shock lined her face. "Noah, is our family going to be destroyed?"

"That's part of what God has been speaking to me about. I've found grace in his eyes and our family is to be spared because I've walked with him."

Mrs. Noah drew a sigh of relief. "But, Noah, what's going to happen? How will God destroy everything?"

"God is planning to send floodwaters and everything on earth will die."

Mothers Who Made a Difference

"What are floodwaters? I've never heard of those before."

"I've never heard of them either, but from what God says, huge amounts of water will cover the earth."

"Noah, how will that happen? I don't understand."

"Dear, sometimes when we can't understand him, we just have to trust him. This is one of those times."

"If the earth will be covered with water, how does God plan to protect our family?"

"Well, that's where the huge piles of wood start to make sense. God has told me to build an ark."

"Noah, what in the world is an ark?" She shook her head. "This just gets stranger and stranger."

"An ark is a vessel that will float on the floodwaters. Our family will be inside and we'll be safe."

"But, Noah, that's a lot of wood you've collected. How big will this ark be?"

"God said to make it 300 cubits long, 50 cubits wide, and 30 cubits high."

Mrs. Noah's mouth dropped open as she tried to imagine the 450-foot long, 75-foot wide, and 45-foot high structure. Her mind couldn't comprehend something so large.

"Noah, why must you build such a big ark for just our family?"

"If the earth will be covered with water, how does God plan to protect our family?"

"Well, that's the other thing I needed to tell you. God's told me to collect a male and a female of all flesh—cattle, birds, animals, creeping things—in order to keep them alive. I'm also supposed to collect seven each of every clean animal. And, of course, we will have to stockpile food for all of us."

Mrs. Noah clasped her head with both hands. "Don't tell me anymore, Noah. I'm on overload right now."

"Honey, that's why I've been praying for God to prepare your heart. I knew this would be a little overwhelming for you."

"A little overwhelming?" Her voice squeaked, hysteria near the surface. "You tell me God's going to destroy the earth using floodwaters that we've never heard of, you've got to build a gigantic ark-thing that will float on those waters, we have to collect and live with two of every creature—including wild animals—and we have to supply food for all of us. And you call that a little overwhelming?"

> *"What if our sons and their wives refuse to go in the ark, Noah?"*

Noah chuckled, pulling her into his arms. "I love you, Mrs. Noah. I know this will take time to sink in. We'll talk again when you're ready. Then we need to discuss this with the children."

A sudden fear hit her. "What if our sons and their

wives refuse to go in the ark, Noah? What will we do? I don't want them to be destroyed."

"Honey, you've prayed for those boys since before they were born. I've seen you on your knees so many times, touching heaven on their behalf. You've been a faithful mother and it won't be for nothing." Noah tenderly stroked her cheek. "We've taught our sons about God, and we've tried our best to live a godly life in front of them. Just pray and leave the situation in God's hands."

> *"Help me to do your will and give my family strength."*

Later that evening, Mrs. Noah knelt to pray. "Jehovah God, this is more than I can comprehend. You know my desire is to serve you. Help me to do your will and give my family strength through this unsettled time. I pray for our sons and daughters-in-law. Don't let our children be swayed by the wickedness of this world." Her tears dripped onto the ground. "Prepare their hearts and help them to be obedient to your leading. I thank you that we can count on your promises—even when we don't understand the circumstances. Amen."

Mrs. Noah was nervous the day Noah told their children about God's judgment and the impending floodwaters, but God had answered her prayers and prepared their hearts.

Mothers Who Made a Difference

Noah and his sons began working on the ark. Soon, the massive size of the vessel began drawing crowds of curious neighbors.

Noah and his family remained faithful to the task God had given them.

"What are you building, Noah?"

"I'm building an ark."

"What in the world is an ark?"

"It's a vessel that will float on floodwaters."

"What are floodwaters?"

"God is grieved by the wickedness of man. He is going to send huge amounts of water to destroy all living things because of their evil lifestyle."

Loud, jeering laughter filled the air. "Noah's gone nuts. Building an ark to float on floodwaters—and he's building it on dry land. He says God's going to destroy us? Get real."

The cruel taunts continued throughout the years Noah and his family worked on the ark. "Hey, Nutty Noah, where's all that water you were talking about? Your ark isn't floating yet! Guess you must have been wrong. By the way, we're still here!"

The ridicule was oppressive but Noah and his family remained faithful to the task God had given them. Noah built the three deck levels and then coated the ark with pitch for waterproofing. Once the rooms were finished, he cut the window and the door, placing them just as God had instructed him.

Mothers Who Made a Difference

While Noah and their sons built the ark, Mrs. Noah and her daughters-in-law stockpiled the food and supplies they would need.

The ark was finally completed and the animals began to arrive, just as God had promised.

Noah put his arm around his wife as the last of the animals entered the ark. "You're an amazing woman, Mrs. Noah. Most wives would have packed their belongings and left the day I came home with that hard-to-believe story about God destroying the earth. They certainly would have left during those years of ridicule and hard work. Yet you remained faithful through all of it." He gave her a heartfelt kiss. "Now let's gather our children. It's our turn to go into the ark."

"You're an amazing woman, Mrs. Noah."

When everyone was on board, Noah stood at the door with one of his sons, taking a final look at the world they had known.

"I'm glad you're here, Son. I'm sure your friends must have tried to lure you into their wicked lifestyle. Weren't you tempted to join them in their wild living?"

"Of course, I was tempted. There were times I gave in to some of those temptations and did things that make me ashamed."

"Your mother and I were worried that you and your wife might choose the pleasures of sin instead of being obedient to God."

He hung his head in shame. "For a while, we considered turning our backs on him. There was so much pressure with everyone making fun of us all the time. And everyone else seemed to be having such a good time the way they were living."

"What made you change your mind?"

"Well, Father, God convicted my heart, and then he gave me peace about this whole situation. You and Mother were also part of my decision. I saw your faithful walk with God and I saw the difference that made in your lives. And there's one other reason."

> *God's grace and their faith led to the salvation of Noah's family.*

"What is that, Son?"

"Never doubt the effectiveness of a mother's prayers. I know I'm here today because my mother prayed for me."

They turned and walked into the ark and God shut the door. As promised, the floodwaters destroyed the earth, but God's grace and their faith led to the salvation of Noah's family.

Application

RUBY AND MRS. NOAH learned the importance of praying for their children. God allowed both mothers the privilege of seeing how their faithfulness influenced the lives of their children.

Ask yourself:

1. Am I willing to trust God even when I can't understand him?
2. Have I planted deep roots spiritually for my child?
3. Have I taught my child to turn to God when the storms of life come?
4. Am I praying faithfully for my child?

Dear heavenly Father,

My heart's desire is to please you. Help my life to be a faithful example to my children. Plant deep roots spiritually in their lives so that they will turn to you whenever the storms of life come their way. Keep them from harm and help them to be obedient to your leading.

Amen.

Reflections

USE THIS SPACE TO RESPOND to the stories or to answer the questions.

_____

_____

_____

_____

_____

_____

_____

_____

_____

_____

_____

_____

_____

Mothers Who Made a Difference

7

Because a
Mother
Left
a
Legacy

A Mother's Story

A WARM BREEZE BLEW across the little church cemetery, carrying with it the sound of children singing "Jesus Loves Me." Tears filled my eyes as I tried to explain to my sons that this was part of their heritage.

When I began researching my husband's family tree, I expected to find dry bones and dusty books. Instead, I found fascinating stories spanning many generations. Finding a spiritual heritage was an unexpected bonus that prompted our visit to the church cemetery that day.

> *Finding a spiritual heritage was an unexpected bonus.*

I led my sons to a crumbling tombstone with fading letters. "Boys, I brought you here because I wanted you to see where your great-great-great-grandmother is buried. Her name was Sareptia Cox and she lived during Civil War times."

"Wow! That was a long time ago," my youngest son said in an awed tone. "Did you know her, Mama?"

I bit back a smile. "No, Son, she died many years before I was born. Her husband, James Cox, was a soldier in the Civil War and he died from battle injuries, leaving her to raise six children by herself. I want to read you the letter that Grandpa James sent to her when he knew he was dying.

Field Hospital, Wilcox Division, Frasier's Farm, June 14, 1864

My Dear Wife,
These few lines will bear to you the sad intelligence that I am severely and perhaps mortally wounded. I was in battle yesterday. I was shot through with a musket ball. The ball entered my left side just under the arm and passed out above the right hip. I have suffered a great deal and am still suffering. I am to be sent to the hospital in Richmond to stay and in all probability this will be the last time you will ever hear from

> *I have suffered a great deal and am still suffering.*

me. Before you receive this, I have no doubt but that I will have exchanged this world of trouble and anxiety for a better one. I want you to meet me in heaven, when it comes your turn to die. If it's the Lord's will that I should be taken now, I am perfectly willing that his will be done, for I feel that I have discharged my duty to my God and to my country. In leaving this world of woe and bloodshed, I am only exchanging it for a better. I want you to raise our children the best you can … I will close [this letter] by again asking you and the dear children to meet me in heaven. And finally, dear wife, farewell.

Your devoted husband,

J. E. Cox

> *I want you to meet me in heaven, when it comes your turn to die.*

"Boys, James and Sareptia Cox left you a special gift. They left you a spiritual heritage. Grandpa James died from his battle wounds, but while he was dying, his last thoughts were about God and meeting his wife and children in heaven. He was a faithful soldier in man's army, but even more important, he was a faithful soldier in God's army. He encouraged Grandma Sareptia to raise the children for the Lord, and that's why we're here today. I want to tell you a

story about her, the ground we're standing on, and the church on the hill behind you.

"Grandma Sareptia granted his request to raise their children for the Lord. I know she did, because nine years later, in 1873, her son Marshall and his wife, Mary—your great-great-grandfather and grandmother—were part of a group of ten people who met to establish a church in their community.

> *"Grandma Sareptia granted his request to raise their children for the Lord."*

"Mary's mother, Lucinda McCrary—your other great-great-great-grandmother—donated the land upon which to build the church, and Grandpa Marshall and another man built the log cabin that served as their first church building."

"That's cool, Mama. Was it a log cabin like on the old *Bonanza* television show?"

"Well, something like that, honey. The common practice in those days was to build the four walls of the cabin and put them in place first. Once they were set, the men would make the door and window openings. Before the door and windows were cut, your grandmother and one of her daughters climbed under the logs and held the first prayer meeting, praying for God's blessings on these grounds and on their community.

"Boys; the brick church behind you is a different building from that log cabin, but this is the church that they helped to establish. The ground we're standing on was donated by your family members, and because of their faithfulness, six generations later, little children are still learning that Jesus loves them. This is your heritage."

The afternoon was special for all of us. My sons were fascinated as they learned about their history, and I was thrilled to share it with them.

That evening as I prepared for bed, I thought about how difficult life must have been for Grandma Sareptia, raising six children by herself, yet she stayed faithful and served God. I, of course, never had the pleasure of meeting her, but six generations later, her life is still casting a shadow of influence on her family and on members of the community where she once lived.

One of the greatest legacies a mother can leave her children is to have lived a godly life in front of them. Grandma Sareptia gave that gift to her children and they in turn passed it down to their children and grandchildren. Now it's my turn—and my responsibility—to leave behind a spiritual legacy for my sons and for future generations.

Please, dear God, help me to be as faithful.

One of the greatest legacies a mother can leave her children is to have lived a godly life in front of them.

We are apt to forget that children watch examples better than they listen to preaching.

—Roy L. Smith

Mothers Who Made a Difference

Straight from Scripture

$\mathcal{T}$ HEN HE CAME TO Derbe and Lystra. And behold, a certain disciple was there, named Timothy, *the* son of a certain Jewish woman who believed, but his father *was* Greek.

He was well spoken of by the brethren who were at Lystra and Iconium.

Paul wanted to have him go on with him. And he took *him* and circumcised him because of the Jews who were in that region, for they all knew that his father was Greek.

And as they went through the cities, they delivered to them the decrees to keep, which were determined by the apostles and elders at Jerusalem.

So the churches were strengthened in the faith, and increased in number daily....

Paul, an apostle of Jesus Christ by the will of God, according to the promise of life which is in Christ Jesus,

To Timothy, a beloved son: Grace, mercy, *and*

peace from God the Father and Christ Jesus our Lord.

I thank God, whom I serve with a pure conscience, as *my* forefathers *did*, as without ceasing I remember you in my prayers night and day, greatly desiring to see you, being mindful of your tears, that I may be filled with joy, when I call to remembrance the genuine faith that is in you, which dwelt first in your grandmother Lois and your mother Eunice, and I am persuaded is in you also....

You therefore, my son, be strong in the grace that is in Christ Jesus.

And the things that you have heard from me among many witnesses, commit these to faithful men who will be able to teach others also.

You therefore must endure hardship as a good soldier of Jesus Christ....

But you must continue in the things which you have learned and been assured of, knowing from whom you have learned *them*, and that from childhood you have known the Holy Scriptures, which are able to make you wise for salvation through faith which is in Christ Jesus. (Acts 16:1–5; 2 Tim. 1:1–5; 2:1–3; 3:14–15)

Mothers Who Made a Difference

Mothers of the Bible

THE BUSTLING SOUNDS of the busy market faded as Eunice climbed to the flat rooftop of her home carrying a pile of blankets and her newborn son. She fashioned a comfortable nest from the blankets and propped the infant, Timothy, where she could see his sweet face.

> "My desire for you is that you will have a holy fear of God all the days of your life."

She kissed his soft cheek. "Oh, Timothy, you are so precious to me and I'm so grateful God has let me be your mother. I know you are just a little baby, and you don't understand this conversation, but there are some things on my heart that I want to tell you."

The baby was still, calmed by the sound of his mother's voice. "From the day I learned you would be joining our family, I've felt that God had something special for you to do when you become a man. Even your name is special. Timothy means 'one who fears God,' and my desire for you is that you will have a holy fear of God all the days of your life."

Eunice adjusted the blanket, sheltering the little one from the breeze that blew across the rooftop. "Timothy, I know you are just a tiny baby, but I want to start teaching you about God. We might as well start at the beginning because God was there at the beginning. He made the light and the darkness. He separated the water from the dry land. He created the grass and the trees, and he hung the stars in the sky. The cattle in the fields and the fish in the sea were all God's creations. Then God created man in his own image. Little one, God created you, and you know what? I think you are one of his best creations. I'll tell you another story about God tomorrow."

Lois climbed the steps to the rooftop, the sound of her daughter's voice becoming clear as she reached the top of the steps. She stopped, listening as Eunice finished telling the story of creation to the tiny baby propped in front of her.

> "God created you, and you know what? I think you are one of his best creations."

"Um … Eunice, he's a newborn baby. I don't think he'll understand those stories yet."

"Well, Mother, I was thinking the other day that I don't know when he will be old enough to understand. I don't want there to ever be a time in his life when he doesn't know about God, so I'm not taking any chances."

Lois gave her daughter a warm hug. "That's a good point, dear. Keep telling those stories. Now, I want to spend some time with my grandson, and I want you to go downstairs to rest for a little while."

"That sounds good, Mother. I didn't realize I was so tired until I sat down."

Eunice walked into the house, but before she stretched out to rest, she knelt beside her bed.

Help him to become a man of character and integrity.

Jehovah God, I thank you for the privilege of being a mother. The responsibility of raising this child sometimes frightens me and I know I can't do it without you. Help me to be the example I should be. Please keep my child safe and keep him from wrong influences. Use his life in a special way. Help him to become a man of character and integrity and give me the wisdom I need to guide this precious child along the road of life. Help me to be faithful in leaving him a spiritual legacy. Amen.

The months turned into years, and the infant became a sturdy toddler who was the joy of Eunice's life. She continued the tradition of telling him stories from God's Word, the practice woven into the fabric of their days as naturally as gathering for family mealtime.

> *Help me to be faithful in leaving him a spiritual heritage.*

When Timothy started putting words together in short sentences, she began teaching him passages of Scripture, and she was awed at the Scripture he memorized over the next few months. She realized he didn't have the passages memorized perfectly, but he was two years old and he already knew that God was in the beginning. As he grew older and his verbal skills increased, she taught him longer passages of Scripture, God's precious promises safely tucked in his heart, ready to retrieve whenever he faced moments of discouragement, fear, or temptation.

As Timothy matured, leaving behind the pudgy-cheeked toddler stage and turning into an active little boy, Eunice continued the habit of praying for her son, kneeling daily beside her bed.

Dear God, some days I feel so incompetent at this job of motherhood. I want to be a good mother more than anything, and yet I seem to fall short on so many occasions. Lord, I need daily guidance and wisdom from you. Please bless my precious child and help him to become a man with a heart that's tender to your leading.

Help me to be faithful in leaving him a spiritual heritage. Amen.

Eunice made a conscious effort to raise her son for the Lord, working diligently to pray with him and to teach him Scripture. What she didn't realize was that her daily example preached an even louder sermon than their daily devotional times.

"Timothy, can you come here, please?"

"Yes, Mother?"

"I've prepared some food for our neighbors. Several of them have been sick and they are going through a rough time right now. Will you help me carry the baskets?"

"Mother, you haven't felt well yourself the last few days. You shouldn't have done all this extra work."

"Son, God has been so good to us. He burdened my heart for our dear friends, and I felt like I was supposed to do this today."

Timothy turned away from her and as he bent to pick up the basket, he swiped the unexpected moisture from his eyes. After all, big boys weren't supposed to cry. *She is such a dear mother. I hope I'm as good a person when I'm grown.*

Eunice was amazed at how swiftly the years passed.

Eunice was amazed at how swiftly the years passed and she was awed by the godly young man her son had become—despite her flaws and imperfections as a mother.

Sometimes during a quiet afternoon, she sat and counted her blessings as she savored the precious memories tucked away in her heart. How she cherished the memories of the times she had walked to the rooftop and found Timothy sitting by himself pondering the Scriptures. The deep, thought-provoking questions he asked had astounded her.

Tears misted her eyes as she thought of the times he had gone alone to the fields to pray. She remembered the afternoon that he came home and she could tell he had been crying. "Timothy, is something wrong, Son?"

She'd remember his words forever. "The Lord touched my heart while I was praying and I just started praising him for all that he has done for me."

How blessed I've been to be his mother.

Eunice was thrilled when he began to travel with the apostle Paul on his missionary journeys. She missed him desperately, but what a precious gift to know that God had answered her prayers and that he could use her son—her beloved Timothy—to share the gospel with a lost and dying world.

> *Tears misted her eyes as she thought of the times he had gone alone to the fields to pray.*

Paul looked at the young man seated across the fire from him. "Timothy, we've traveled together for many months now and you've become like a son to me. I'm grateful God sent you to help me. I've often thought how unusual it is to see a young man so tender towards the things of God. I know he has done a special work in your heart and you give him all the glory. But what else do you think made the difference in your life and why are you so committed to serving him?"

> *"One of the reasons I'm the man I am today is because of my mother."*

"I've thought about that before. One of the reasons I'm the man I am today is because of my mother. From the time I was an infant, she told me stories from God's Word and taught me passages of Scripture. She lived a life that was an example of what a godly person should be, and she prayed for me."

He paused for a moment, unable to speak around the lump in his throat. "I can't tell you the times I passed through the house and heard my mother talking to God about me. Paul, she spent so much time on her knees in prayer that I think she must have worn grooves into the floor beside her bed. Just think how I'd be letting my mother down if I wasn't a faithful soldier in God's army."

He wiped a stray tear that had escaped down his

cheek. "You know, one of the greatest legacies a mother can leave her children is to have lived a godly life in front of them. That's the special heritage my mother's given me and now it's my turn—and my responsibility—to leave behind a spiritual legacy for future generations.

Application

SAREPTIA AND EUNICE both faced the fearsome responsibility of raising their children for the Lord. Both lived their lives in a manner that left a spiritual legacy for their children and future generations, and as a result, they had the pleasure of watching as their children became adults who loved and served God.

Ask yourself:

1. What am I doing to leave behind a spiritual legacy for my child?
2. How does my daily life affect my child?
3. What steps can I take to become a better example to my child?
4. Have I made the effort to teach my child God's Word?

Dear God,

I thank you for the privilege of being a mother. The responsibility of raising this child sometimes frightens me and I know I can't do it without you. Help me to be the example I should be. Please keep my child safe and away from wrong influences. Use this remarkable life in a special way. Help my child to become a person of character and integrity and give me the wisdom I need to guide this precious being along the road of life. Help me to be faithful in leaving my loved one a spiritual legacy.

Amen.

Reflections

USE THIS SPACE TO RESPOND to the stories or to answer the questions.

_____

_____

_____

_____

_____

_____

_____

_____

_____

_____

_____

_____

8

Because a Mother Rocked a Baby

A Mother's Story

THE SADNESS in Pat's eyes broke my heart. Our families were on vacation together. While our husbands and my sons played golf, the two of us hit the outlet mall. We had browsed through several shops when I noticed the baby store across the sidewalk. "Oh good, there's a baby store. I need to buy a gift."

"I'll wait on you," she responded quietly. "I don't go in baby stores. It's just too painful and I don't do that to myself anymore."

Tears filled my eyes as I walked into the store. Prior to the birth of my sons, I had also experienced the heart-breaking pain of infertility. Those were the longest years of my life.

> *Prior to the birth of my sons, I had also experienced the heart-breaking pain of infertility.*

Long-buried memories surfaced, and I remembered the agony of having my hopes dashed every month. I thought of the well-meaning friends who asked, "When are you and Paul going to start a family?" never knowing that their words stabbed me in the heart. I remembered the pain I felt while attending baby showers for all of my friends, and the guilt I felt because their joy made me sad. And I remembered holding their babies and then going home in tears because my own arms were empty.

> *I'll never forget the joy of finally holding my baby boy in my arms for the first time.*

I'll never forget the joy of finally holding my baby boy in my arms for the first time, his arrival made even sweeter because I thought I'd never have children. How I wished my dear friend could have known that joy.

Pat and her husband Tad were perfect parent material. She was gentle and kind; he was a popular youth pastor. They had devoted their lives to loving and teaching other people's children. It was such a shame they couldn't have their own. After nineteen years of marriage, I thought they had given up hoping for a child—until that day.

I couldn't quit thinking about Pat's comment. The sadness in her eyes haunted me. Later that

evening I told my husband, "I'm going to ask God to send a child for Tad and Pat. Even if it's not a baby, there's surely a child out there somewhere who needs someone to love them."

"Honey," my husband replied, "they've both just turned forty. I don't think they'd want a child at their age."

"You didn't see Pat's face today. I'm going to pray for a child."

Several months later, Pat and I went to lunch. As we drove home, she started crying. "I've got to tell you something. One of the girls in the youth group has a sister with serious problems and she's pregnant. With her circumstances, there's no way she can keep the baby, but it's important to her to know that her child will go to a home where he or she will be loved and taught about God. Her family asked if we would be interested in adoption. We've prayed about it and … we're going to adopt the baby. Are we crazy?"

"We've prayed about it and … we're going to adopt the baby. Are we crazy?"

I was crying so hard I could barely see to drive. "Pat, I've been praying since our vacation for God to send you a child. This is even more wonderful than what I imagined. I never dreamed he would send you a newborn baby. Isn't God good?"

Mothers Who Made a Difference

"I'm so excited, but … what if I'm … not a good mother?"

"Pat, if God's not worried about your ability to be a good mother, why should you worry? Whenever God gives us something to do, he always equips us with what we need to accomplish that task and he will equip you with the skills you need to be a good mother."

The next few months were filled with joyous anticipation as those dreams Pat had once thought packed away forever, were taken out, dusted off, and polished with hope.

I had the privilege of shopping with Pat on her first visit to a baby store. Tears of joy filled her eyes as she looked at car seats and picked out sheets and diapers. "Oh, isn't this adorable?" She smoothed the soft fabric of a pair of pajamas as she hugged them close. "I can't believe I'm finally going to be a mother. Can you believe Tad and I are going to have a baby in our house?"

"Can you believe Tad and I are going to have a baby in our house?"

The weeks until the due date flew by as they prepared the nursery and finalized all the legal details. Tyler Hudson Marshall was born—quite appropriately—on Thanksgiving Day, and Tad and

Pat took their little miracle home from the hospital knowing that *nothing* is too hard for the Lord.

"If God's not worried about your ability to be a good mother, why should you worry?"

No man has ever tested the resources of God until he tries what is humanly impossible.
—F. B. Meyer

Straight from Scripture

*T*HEN THE LORD appeared to him by the terebinth trees of Mamre, as he was sitting in the tent door in the heat of the day.

So he lifted his eyes and looked, and behold, three men were standing by him; and when he saw *them*, he ran from the tent door to them, and bowed himself to the ground, and said, "My Lord, if I have now found favor in Your sight, do not pass on by Your servant.

"Please let a little water be brought, and wash your feet, and rest yourselves under the tree.

"And I will bring a morsel of bread, that you may refresh your hearts. After that you may pass by, inasmuch as you have come to your servant." They said, "Do as you have said."

So Abraham hurried into the tent to Sarah and said, "Quickly, make ready three measures of fine meal; knead *it* and make cakes."

And Abraham ran to the herd, took a tender and

good calf, gave *it* to a young man, and he hastened to prepare it.

So he took butter and milk and the calf which he had prepared, and set *it* before them; and he stood by them under the tree as they ate.

Then they said to him, "Where *is* Sarah your wife?" So he said, "Here, in the tent."

And He said, "I will certainly return to you according to the time of life, and behold, Sarah your wife shall have a son." (Sarah was listening in the tent door which *was* behind him.)

Now Abraham and Sarah were old, well advanced in age; *and* Sarah had passed the age of childbearing.

Therefore Sarah laughed within herself, saying, "After I have grown old, shall I have pleasure, my lord being old also?"

And the LORD said to Abraham, "Why did Sarah laugh, saying, 'Shall I surely bear *a child*, since I am old?'

"Is anything too hard for the LORD? At the appointed time I will return to you, according to the time of life, and Sarah shall have a son."

But Sarah denied *it*, saying, "I did not laugh," for she was afraid. And He said, "No, but you did laugh!" ...

And the LORD visited Sarah as He had said, and the LORD did for Sarah as He had spoken.

For Sarah conceived and bore Abraham a son in

his old age, at the set time of which God had spoken to him.

And Abraham called the name of his son who was born to him—whom Sarah bore to him—Isaac.

Then Abraham circumcised his son Isaac when he was eight days old, as God had commanded him.

Now Abraham was one hundred years old when his son Isaac was born to him.

And Sarah said, "God has made me laugh, *and* all who hear will laugh with me." (Gen. 18:1–15; 21:1–6)

Mothers of the Bible

I MUSTN'T LAUGH *out loud*, Sarah thought. Laughter bubbled to the surface anyway, threatening to overflow as she tried to regain control. She wiped the tears from her cheeks and then clamped both hands over her mouth in a heroic effort to silence the peals of hysterical laughter. After all, she

> *What they had said was so funny!*

didn't want to offend their special guests, and she didn't want them to know she'd been eavesdropping—but what they had said was so funny!

The sun glaring off the desert sand made the heat in the tent almost unbearable. Sarah hadn't meant to listen to the men, but the doorway of the tent was the only place to catch an occasional breeze. Having completed her tasks, she settled there to rest, her mind drifting back to the hectic events of the last few hours.

Abraham had burst into the tent, causing Sarah to smile at his obvious excitement as he exclaimed, "Honey, I need your help."

"Well, of course, dear. Why are you so excited?"

"Sarah, the Lord is here, and he's brought two men with him. I've fetched some water so they can wash up and rest a little while under the shade tree. Can you get some of your finest meal and bake three special cakes on the hearth?"

"Of course, Abraham. What else should I prepare?"

"Don't worry about the rest. I'll get my finest calf from the herd and have one of the young men prepare it. With fresh milk and some of the wonderful butter you churned yesterday, that should make a delicious feast."

Sarah is going to have a son.

The morning's flurry of activity combined with the intense midday heat had made Sarah tired. With the men enjoying their meal, she had almost dozed off when she heard one of the men ask, "Where is Sarah, your wife?"

"Oh, she's in the tent."

Then she heard the Lord say, "I know Sarah is physically past the age where she can have children, but I'm going to return that time of life to her, and Sarah is going to have a son."

That's the point where the giggles had overtaken her. *I'm ninety years old and Abraham's one hundred years old—and we're going to have a child?* The thought was so crazy she couldn't do anything but laugh.

A few moments later, she sobered instantly as the Lord said, "Why did Sarah laugh?"

She sat there in stunned silence, her mind whirling. She buried her head in her hands, a silent prayer moving her lips. "God, don't do this to me. Don't give me hope where there is none. You know I packed those dreams away when it became impossible for me to bear a child. You

> *"Is anything too hard for the Lord?"*

know how I grieved. You know the shame I felt when I was unable to give Abraham the son he wanted. Oh, God, you know the pain of my empty arms, the sorrow I felt when my friends rejoiced at the births of their babies—and the guilt I felt because their joy brought me sadness. Why would you be so cruel as to give me hope when I'm too old to bear a child?"

Then she heard the Lord's voice again. "Is anything too hard for the Lord? When it's my chosen time, you shall have a son."

Tears filled her eyes as the hair on her arms stood

up. *Could … it … really happen?* A peace she couldn't explain filled her soul. Dropping to her knees, she worshipped, her tears dripping and pooling in the sandy soil. "God, this seems so impossible to me, but as I've walked with you throughout the years, you've proven time and time again that what seems impossible to me is so possible for you. I don't understand how you're going to accomplish this, but I trust you."

> *"I don't understand how you're going to accomplish this, but I trust you."*

Her hand stroked the flatness of her abdomen, her mind imagining a baby growing there. *We're going to have a baby!* And, in that moment of trust, those dreams Sarah had once thought packed away forever were taken out, dusted off, and polished with hope.

Months passed, and then one day Abraham arrived home to find Sarah waiting for him, tears streaming down her cheeks.

He took her in his arms. "Honey, what's wrong? Please tell me why you're so upset. You know I can't stand to see you cry." He tenderly brushed the tears from her cheeks.

"Abraham, these aren't tears of sadness. I'm so happy I can't contain it. The Lord's chosen time has arrived just as he said it would. After all those years of sadness and barrenness, we're going to have a

182   *Mothers Who Made a Difference*

baby! Did you hear me? *You're going to be a father!*" Sarah twirled around the tent in excitement. "I've suspected it for the last few weeks and I've been about to pop trying to keep it a secret until I was sure. Abraham, we're finally going to hold a baby in our arms! Isn't God amazing? Oh, my goodness, what are we doing just standing here? We have to get busy. We're going to have a baby!"

Joyous laughter filled the tent as the two of them celebrated, making plans and dreaming of the son they would soon welcome to their family. "Abraham, I wonder what he'll look like. He'll be so handsome if he looks like you." She wrapped her arms around his neck. "Just imagine, we'll hear a child's laughter in this tent and the sound of little feet skipping through the desert sand. Oh honey, just think, you can teach our son how to ride a camel and how to find water in the desert. Why, nine months is going to seem like forever!"

The months progressed and then the doubts and fears—and hormones—that every new mother experiences began to surface. In the still darkness of the night, Abraham thought he heard a quiet sniffle.

"Honey, are you okay? Is something bothering you?"

Joyous laughter filled the tent as the two of them celebrated.

"Well … now that it's obvious I'm going to have a child, everyone will be talking about us, and you know how I hate that," Sarah said, "What will we say when people ask about it?"

"Well, my love, we'll tell them what they should have already known—that every child is a miracle from God, and we just had to wait a little longer than normal for our miracle to get here."

"Okay. But, Abraham … what if I'm … not a good mother?"

"Sarah, our son is a gift from the Lord. If God's not worried about your ability to be a good mother, why should you worry? Whenever God gives us something to do, he always equips us with what we need to accomplish that task."

With a deep sigh of relief, Sarah said, "Thank you, Abraham, I think I can sleep now."

Love for this tiny child overwhelmed her.

Finally, the time arrived and their long-awaited son was born. Sarah cuddled her little miracle in her arms, kissing his chubby toes, and stroking his soft hair. Love for this tiny child overwhelmed her, his birth even more precious because she had once thought she'd never know the joy of becoming a mother.

Snuggling the baby on her shoulder, she whispered,

"I love you, little one. Your father and I have waited such a long time for you to get here. We'd given up hope, but here you are in my arms." She wiped a tear from her cheek. "You're too little to understand yet, but you're our miracle child, and we gave you a special name—Isaac. Your name means 'laughter' and you are God's gift of joy and laughter to us. Oh, Son, I have so much I want to teach you about life and God, but there's one important lesson I plan to teach you every day of your life: *Nothing* is too hard for the Lord."

> *"You're too little to understand yet, but you're our miracle child."*

Application

*P*AT AND SARAH both experienced the pain of infertility and the sadness of longing for a child. When God granted their desire and gave them a baby under seemingly impossible circumstances, they both learned the valuable lesson that nothing is too hard for the Lord.

Ask yourself:

1. Do I often feel inadequate as a mother?
2. Have I brought my fears to the Lord and asked for his help?
3. What circumstances am I facing that seem impossible to me?
4. Have I learned yet that "nothing is too hard for the Lord"?

Dear Lord,

I'm grateful that nothing is too hard for you. Thank you for always being there for me during the difficult times of my life. Thank you for answering prayer when I face circumstances that seem impossible to me. Thank you for giving me the gift of being a mother. Equip me with the skills I need to be the mother that you want me to become.

Amen.

Reflections

USE THIS SPACE TO RESPOND to the stories or to answer the questions.

_____

_____

_____

_____

_____

_____

_____

_____

_____

_____

_____

_____

_____

_____

_____

_____

_____

_____

_____

_____

_____

_____

_____

_____

_____

_____

_____

_____

_____

_____

_____

_____

_____

_____

Mothers Who Made a Difference

Sources

A Harmony of the Life of Jesus: Jerusalem at the Time of Christ. *The Bible Knowledge Accelerator*, 1995–1996.

http://www.bible-history.com/jesus/jesusJerusalem_at_the_Time_of_Christ.htm. Accessed January 2, 2006.

Cox, James E. [Civil War Letter to Wife]. 14 June 1864. Cox Family History File, Henderson County Genealogical Society, Hendersonville, NC.

Jones, George Alexander. *The Heritage of Henderson County North Carolina* Volume 1 1985. Winston-Salem: Hunter Publishing Company, 1985.

Kelly, Bob. *Worth Repeating: More Than 5,000 Classic and Contemporary Quotes*. Grand Rapids: Kregel Publications, 2003.

Lockyer, Herbert. *All the Women of the Bible*. Grand Rapids: Zondervan, 1967.